"In a completely rational society, the best of us would aspire to be teachers, and the rest of us would have to settle for something less; because passing civilization on from one generation to the next ought to be the highest honor and responsibility anyone could have."

—— Lee Iaccoca

WHAT TEACHERS ARE SAYING ABOUT
EDUCATION FOR TRANSFORMATION

"I have learned to be a Masterful Listener. As a result, I have been able to be more open with my students. to take their feelings into consideration, to empathize and be a better person and a better teacher."
Arlan Martin, Teacher, Academy of Environmental Sciences, New York City

"I learned that it's my responsibility to make the classroom a caring and homelike environment for the children."
Sam Campiformio, Middle School 229, Queens, New York

"This book has been very useful to me, because it has taught me that by taking better care of myself I am taking better care of my students."
Donna Foster, Middle School 180, Bronx, New York

"I choose peace over war and all the techniques to establish this peace. Since I began using the information from your book with my students, the atmosphere in my class has become much more peaceful."
Shirley Thomas, Middle School 144, Bronx, New York

"Prior to reading this book, l was a selective listener. In other words I listened to what I wanted to listen to. Now I am learning and practicing listening to others without interrupting. This has changed my life."
Carolyn Frazier, Middle School 113, Bronx, New York

"The words Create, Promote, Allow, are something everyone already knows, but we just don't recognize it in our life. Once we take control, once we feel we are responsible for everything that happens, then we have a part in it. If we face that first as opposed to blaming, we will succeed. This is very powerful."
Marc Etienne, teacher, New York Family Academy, New York City

EDUCATION
FOR
TRANSFORMATION

**CREATING HEALTHY RELATIONSHIPS WITH OUR STUDENTS
THROUGH PERSONAL TRANSFORMATION**

BY

DR. MARC ROSENBAUM

ISBN: 0-9753540-1-9

EDUCATION FOR TRANSFORMATION

CONTENTS

ACKNOWLEDGMENTS

I am eternally grateful to four of my mentors: Seymour Fliegel, Dr. Harvey Kaye, Jamal Young and Dr. Anthony Palomeni. They saw value in my work and gave me the opportunity to present my programs before it was popular to do so.

Thanks to Cheryl Lugo and my dear friends Heide Banks and Howard Lazar for their valuable advice and ongoing support. I would also like to thank the teachers who gave me the knowledge and spiritual insight that made it possible for me to grow and eventually share what I have learned. Thanks to Fritz Perls, Oscar Ichazo and Swami Muktananda who, at the beginning of my search, awakened me to experiencing that I was more than my mind, body and emotions. A special thank you to Melba Alhonte who has become a cherished friend as well as an invaluable collaborator. Thanks also to Drs. Ron and Mary Hulnick, the presidents of the University of Santa Monica, and to John-Roger who taught me and continues to teach me how to practically apply my earlier wisdom in the world while becoming a more loving and compassionate human being.

PROLOGUE

I have found that the best way to teach children to learn and assimilate the knowledge, skills and behavior that will allow them to be successful in the world is to educate the people who have the greatest influence on their lives: their parents and teachers. The first step in this transformation is to change from being obsessed with our students' behavior to becoming aware of and responsible for own behavior.

In 1992, I left a highly successful twenty-year career as a dental surgeon to pursue my vision of teaching children personal transformation. This vision had its inception in a childhood where I was taught very little about the consequences of my actions or how to effectively deal with others' needs. Until I learned and practiced specific social and emotional principles, I was often in trouble and engaged in disruptive and unfulfilling relationships.

Thirty years ago, in an effort to deal with my problems, I began to explore the teachings of various spiritual traditions and to study with several leading practitioners in the human potential movement. This gave me the impetus to pursue a Masters of Education in theology and to earn a Masters in Applied Psychology. Slowly but surely, over many years, I've learned how to be truly happy and function as a more effective, conscious and loving human being.

The journey of self-exploration was the most important choice I ever made. If only I had learned as a child how to take responsibility for my life and to recognize, understand and effectively deal with my emotions — instead of always blaming others for my suffering — my early years might have been far less painful and more productive. This life changing exploration motivated me to create the Self-Mastery program based on the premise that in order to be an effective teacher, parent or student, we must first be an effective human being.

During twelve years of presenting the Self-Mastery program to more than 4000 students, parents and teachers, I have I found that the quality of the participants' lives improves as they explore options, such as taking responsibility rather than blaming others, forgiving instead of harboring feelings of hatred or resentment, assertively communicating rather than being habitually passive or aggressive, and having empathy and acceptance rather than judging themselves and others.

Education for Transformation is not about presenting the latest "techniques" that are guaranteed to bring classroom bliss. This is a practical manual designed to educate, motivate and lead you through a series of precise exercises that show you how your attitudes, beliefs and behaviors affect your students. As you learn to truly serve yourself, you will become a guiding light for your students and become the best teacher you can possibly be.

You can learn a great deal by just reading this book. But, along with your reading, if you also complete the exercises, I promise you a new world of personal transformation and professional satisfaction.

INTRODUCTION

EDUCATION FOR TRANSFORMATION

In order for change to be significant, teaching must be approached at the level of an individual transformation that requires courage and commitment.

This book is not about teaching the latest "techniques" that, when used correctly, will end every problem that an educator faces. Instead, the emphasis is on increasing the performance of students by raising the overall effectiveness of the teacher. To be effective teachers, we must transform ourselves from being obsessed with our students' behavior to becoming aware of and responsible for our own behavior.

We often find ourselves frustrated by our students' apathy, troublesome behavior, destructive habits and inconsistent academic performance. In many cases, conflict and alienation have replaced our vision of a relationship based on mutual caring, cooperation, trust and respect. This disharmony in our schools is being mirrored in society by escalating crime, pregnancy, suicide and drug and alcohol abuse rates among our youth. As teachers we search for answers.

WHAT IS THE SOLUTION?

It's easy to blame an administration we believe to be unjust, parents whom we judge as not caring enough, and today's children for their alleged apathy. However, there is a more responsible explanation for the discord in our families and society – one that provides us not only with hope but also with the tools to reverse the trend.

The answer lies in education, a type of education that develops the intelligence that has been shown to improve our health, relationships, academic performance and the achievement of our goals. It is the intelligence that gives us the ability to observe and reflect on the relationship we have with ourselves, others and the world around us before taking action. It is the intelligence that, when developed, leads us to make choices that better serve ourselves and others and prepares us to deal with life and its challenges more effectively.

This intelligence goes beyond the ability to memorize facts. We have spent years of education focusing on math, science, reading, writing – even dancing, drawing and athletics. But in order for our students to become truly knowledgeable, responsible and caring human beings, we must teach social and emotional principles with the same structure and attention that has been devoted to traditional subjects.

WE CANNOT GIVE WHAT WE NEVER GOT

In an ideal world this necessary social and emotional learning would be an integral part of our children's schooling. But most schools do not have the resources, time or qualified instructors to effectively teach this type of intelligence. In most instances, the only place a child can receive this type of education is in the home.

After several years of presenting the Self-Mastery program to students, I observed that many of them would demonstrate valued principles in their lives only to have them not supported at home. As a result, they often returned to prior negative habits. But parents cannot teach what they do not know. Some were fortunate enough to have emotionally intelligent parents as role models, but most were not. How can parents demonstrate compassion, forgiveness, acceptance, communication and listening skills if they were never taught how to incorporate these qualities into their lives? It's as ludicrous as asking students to solve a complicated math problem without ever teaching them basic arithmetic.

We have consistently found that the best way to foster social-emotional learning for children is to educate the people who have the greatest influence on their lives: their parents and teachers. For this reason, approximately 80 percent of the Self-Mastery courses are now being presented to parents and teachers. For those children who do not have socially and emotionally intelligent parents, you the teacher, may be the only person in their lives to demonstrate the qualities that are the foundation for becoming a productive member of society.

THE ESSENTIAL TOOL IS AWARENESS

The foundation of social-emotional intelligence is the ability to be aware of our thoughts, actions and feelings as they occur. By looking at ourselves in the present moment without judgment, we see how our attitudes and behavior affect us and everyone else in our lives. As we develop the ability to be aware, we discover patterns in our responses to certain situations. These patterns or habitual reactions are automatic, predictable and almost always inappropriate. They are the primary source of the pain that we cause ourselves and others.

For example, a course participant shared a story about the time she was waiting with her husband and their five children for their plane to depart. The flight was canceled and rescheduled to a nearby airport. Upon their arrival at the other airport, that plane was canceled. She spoke about how she would usually get upset and find someone to yell at. This time, after taking a moment to be aware of her habitual response, she was able to remain calm by consciously reflecting on the futility of being upset in this situation.

Through awareness, we discover that we have more choices than we realize. We come to see, perhaps for the first time, what is best for ourselves and before long we develop the ability to see what really is best for our students as well as others in our lives. Awareness makes it possible to respond to life and its challenges with openness and compassion rather than being controlled by habitual behavior patterns.

THE 13 PRINCIPLES OF SELF-MASTERY

With awareness as the foundation, there are 13 principles of self-mastery to embody on the path to becoming masterful teachers. Embodying these principles is a two-fold process: First, we must learn them and second, we must adopt them as the basis of our relationship with our students. When we integrate these principles into our daily lives, everyone benefits. The 13 principles of self-mastery are:

1. There is Always a Choice

2. Listen Before You Leap

3. Take Care of Yourself

4. Reflect Before You Act

5. Practice Acceptance and Empathy Rather than Judgment

6. Take Responsibility Rather Than Blaming Others

7. Forgive Rather than Taking Revenge

8. Be Kind Instead of Being Cruel

9. Communicate Lovingly Rather than Aggressively or Passively

10. Use Mistakes as Opportunities to Grow Instead of Reasons To Punish Yourself

11. Show Gratitude Whenever Possible

12. Observe and Change Irrational Beliefs and Destructive habits

13. Love Always Heals

We teach who we are. As we demonstrate these principles in our lives, our students have a direct experience of them and absorb them into their view of themselves and the world around them. When we speak in a calm voice, our students learn how to stay composed when provoked. When we take responsibility for being late or acting inappropriately, we teach our students the role they play in determining what their life looks like at any particular moment. When we give our students positive feedback for a job well done, we are teaching them the power and self-esteem that comes from being acknowledged.

GUIDE TO EFFECTIVELY USING THIS BOOK

Over the twelve years in which I've presented the Self-Mastery programs, I have seen the lives of hundreds of teachers transformed. My vision for this book is to inspire and help a wider audience to live a more rewarding life — a life in which serving ourselves and those we interact with becomes an ongoing commitment.

Whether you are enrolled in a Education for Transformation Program or are reading this book without the benefit of classroom support, I cannot stress enough the importance of doing the home assignments. The exercises and home assignments will promote remarkable changes in your life and the lives of those around you, but again, you have to do them in order to reap the benefits. I suggest that you read one chapter at a time — ideally one per week — just as we do in the classroom. As you do the home assignments, it's a good idea to reread the chapter so that the material remains fresh in your mind. Ideally, you should complete one full chapter, including the home assignment, before going on to the next chapter. How much effort you devote to this process is your choice, but I can tell you from experience that those participants who are really committed derive the greatest benefit.

Also, feel free to write your own notes and experiences in the margins.

THE COMMITMENT — GOING FOR MASTERY

As the Education for Transformation program unfolds, I often hear participants exclaim, "This work is hard!" It is hard. It's easy to get angry, not listen and resist change. The quest for mastery can be frustrating, because you're observing and trying to transform patterns that have been reinforced over many years. For most of us, being judgmental or unforgiving has become second nature: it's not easy to accept and change that in ourselves. I encourage you to be gentle with yourself as you go through this journey. Be patient, but persevere. This book will help you to attain mastery over your life. That's a big project. It's bound to be an uphill battle at times. But the rewards come in direct proportion to the effort and commitment that you invest. As you complete each step thoroughly, you'll see the results of what you've learned, in yourself and in your relationship with others, especially your students.

1

YOU ALWAYS HAVE A CHOICE

Masterful teaching is a process of consciously choosing the most appropriate action in any given situation — the appropriate action being the one that provides the best possible experience for yourself and your students.

We are always making choices. Almost everything we think, say or do represents a choice. And ideally, everything we thought, did or said would provide the best possible outcome for ourselves and others. But too often our choices are not choices at all, but unconscious reactions based on past conditioning or social pressures. We look at the world through an accumulation of attitudes, opinions, and tastes imposed on us by outside influences. Our parents, our teachers, our peers — even TV, movies and magazines — have all played their part in shaping our view of the world. There is very little we think, do or say that isn't a direct result of our past conditioning.

We rarely view the world with the freshness and innocence of a young child. When someone leans over a baby's crib, the baby doesn't think, "What an ugly blouse," or "I don't like red curly hair," or "He's too fat," or "I don't know if I can trust this guy." An infant's view of the world hasn't been tainted by judgments or comparisons.

Upon closer inspection, even if we think we're making choices, often we are allowing our past conditioning and society's mores to choose for us. Who decided when it was suddenly fashionable for women to wear sneakers to work after decades of wearing high heels everyday? Who gave men permission to wear earrings after it was previously perceived as feminine? Who said that baggy pants and loose clothing were fashionable for kids when 30 years ago as teenagers we wore tight pants and pointy shoes? Did individuals or the media decide for us?

13

When we make a choice, we need to look at who or what is influencing our decision. I realized after practicing dentistry for several years that it did not suit my personality or talents. I had decided that I wanted to be a dentist at the ripe old age of thirteen. In reality it was my parents, the influence of society and my Jewish culture which decided that dentistry would be a fine profession for me.

WHO IS IN CONTROL OF YOUR LIFE?

Most psychologists agree that the values and beliefs we absorb during the first seven years of life, mostly from our parents and teachers, determine how we see ourselves and how we relate to others for the rest of our lives. When we are children, our parents are like gods. We accept everything they say and do as the gospel truth. When parents treat their children lovingly and make them feel valued, self-worth becomes the foundation of the child's development. If, on the other hand, children are denied love and attention during their formative years, the chances of them developing a healthy sense of self-esteem are greatly diminished.

Most negative attitudes and fears are created by painful memories from our early childhood experience. Sexual abuse during childhood can manifest as sexual dysfunction. Fear of abandonment can become jealousy. A child's negative self-image can become the source of dysfunction, such as phobias, anorexia, obesity or substance abuse.

How do we overcome the effects of negative conditioning in ourselves? First, we have to acknowledge that past experience determines our present thoughts, attitudes, beliefs and fears. **Only when we acknowledge the influence of past conditioning can we develop the power to suspend those thoughts, attitudes, beliefs and fears.** The following story, told by a course participant, illustrates this point:

"When I first began dating my wife, an incident occurred that dramatically influenced the course of our relationship. We were both feeling very loving toward each other, when I said something to her in a joking manner. The next thing I knew, she hauled off and slapped me.

Although it was not my intention, she thought that I was I was teasing her. After discussing the incident, she saw that my words triggered the anger she'd felt but never expressed when, as a little girl, she was teased by her two older brothers."

Extreme emotional responses usually have very little to do with what is actually happening in the moment. If we look at ourselves honestly, we see that out of balance emotions are almost always triggered by events from our past that we haven't yet resolved. Until we realize that we have a choice in the matter — that we can actually select our thoughts through reflection and observation — we will inevitably rerun the same old patterns over and over again.

Let me give you a couple of examples from my own life. Several years ago I was involved in a lengthy process of buying an apartment. Whenever I heard my lawyer's voice on the answering machine, my first thought was to assume that something was wrong. I remained upset until I was able to speak with her and find out that nothing catastrophic had happened. In fact, she often had good news for me!

This tendency to expect the worst operated in many areas of my life. For example, if I had a dinner appointment with a friend and the friend left a message on my answering machine to call back, my first thought was that the dinner had been canceled. In these situations, my responses were as habitual and automatic as Pavlov's dog and the emotions they evoked were quite painful.

I knew that negative thinking like this came from somewhere in my past. I had been unconsciously repeating this pattern for years. But once I began observing my fears and anxiety, I saw that I could choose to let go of the old pattern. Now when anxiety-provoking thoughts arise, I usually dismiss them as thoughts that don't serve me. Through self-awareness, I am better able to access information that more accurately reflects the reality of a current situation. As a result I feel much better about myself. I also do not experience the physical pain that often resulted from the negative thoughts and emotions.

15

FEELINGS FOLLOW THOUGHT

A man sees a snake lying on the ground at a distance in front of him. He becomes frightened and runs away screaming, "Snake! Snake!" Another man, observing the situation from a closer vantage point, said, "Don't be afraid. That's not a snake. It's just a piece of rope lying on the ground." The first man's fear was real, though the snake was not. The feeling (fear) followed the thought (snake).

In other words, what we think determines what we feel. Anorexics get upset because they think that weighing 90 pounds is too fat. We get angry at someone's behavior because we think they **should know better.** We pace the floor because our son is 15 minutes late and we think that something horrible has happened to him. We react defensively when we think that our authority is being threatened.

Every thought we have sends electrical signals through our brain. This, in turn, influences the limbic system (structures deep in our brains), which, depending upon the nature of the stimulation, translates our emotional state into a range of physical feelings from relaxation or tension. Dr. Mark George of the National Institute of Health determined that happy thoughts cool off the limbic system, whereas sad thoughts cause a significant increase in deep limbic activity. Through this mechanism, our thoughts significantly influence every cell in our bodies.

The deep limbic portion of our brain not only allows us to experience and express emotions, but also stores past emotional experiences. Whenever we remember a particular event, our brain releases chemicals similar to those released when we originally experienced the event. An example would be a rape victim who has an emotionally based physical reaction whenever she sees a man who has a physical characteristic in common with her attacker. Similarly, people who had little bonding with their parents have a negative chemical imprint in their brain. Whenever someone looks at them the wrong way, it triggers the same chemical patterns in the brain as in the earlier negative experiences.

Conversely, thinking positive thoughts cools down the limbic system and can lessen the irritability and depression caused by an overactive limbic structure. **Exercise is another, extremely effective, way to send** blood to the deep limbic structures that are responsible for calming the emotions. In addition, protein has been proven essential for maintaining the health of the deep limbic structures. For this reason, protein snacks, such as cheese or poultry, are usually preferable to sugary snacks, which can promote moodiness, lethargy and lack of focus.

STINKING THINKING

Given the thought-emotion connection, it would be a wonderful world if most of the thoughts we have were positive and thus produced a soothing emotional state. Unfortunately this is not the case. Researchers have measured that more than 70 percent of the thoughts we have are not beneficial to ourselves or others. Many of the negative thoughts we have are habitual and automatic. Moreover, not all thoughts are accurate or prove to be true when tested in reality. Thoughts that have the words always, never, no one, everyone, every time, etc. in them are usually not accurate. "He's always putting me down." "I'll never get a raise." "My children never listen to me." Such ideas are inaccurate, but nevertheless stimulate the limbic structure. Also, negative categories of thoughts, such as focusing on the negative ("He will probably never call"), labeling yourself or someone else ("He's just a liar"), personalizing ("He seems angry, I must have done something wrong"), blaming ("I had nothing to do with the argument," "I couldn't help it," "It's all your fault") and worrying about the past or future stimulate the limbic structure and produce varying degrees of physical stress.

Most negative thoughts are habitual and go unnoticed. But even though they may not be noticed by our mind at a conscious level, they are taken in by our bodies in the form of physical tension. We will suffer the effects of our negative thoughts until we realize we have a choice: to be brought down by our own negativity or to move in a positive direction. While that sounds very neat and simple in theory, how does it work in reality?

Let's say you have a habit of becoming angry and yelling when your spouse is emotionally upset and withdraws his or her affection. One day you come to a point where you begin **observing this process rather than reacting in a habitually negative manner.** With this new awareness, you understand that your spouse's emotional ups and downs don't necessarily have anything to do with you, are not your fault and certainly don't imply that your spouse is about to leave you. Once you have this understanding, you can try to identify why you tend to react the way you do. Reflecting on your childhood, you may notice a pattern whereby your parents led you to feel that you were to blame for their emotional upset. Or you may ask, "Who else, besides my spouse, has made me feel badly when they were out of balance?" Or, when did you associate someone being upset with you with meaning they were going to leave you?

Think about the times you've reacted with anger to someone else's emotional imbalance. Did your reaction ever do any good? Probably not. Probably never. So try an experiment. The next time your spouse gets upset, try to react with empathy rather than anger. See whether it makes a difference. And if a week later your spouse becomes moody and the same old pattern kicks in again - you get angry and yell - don't despair and beat up on yourself. Just be aware of your reactions and resolve to do things differently the next time.

DON'T BE CRUEL

We can consciously choose our response to every situation that is presented. Yet, there are instances where we suffer because we react habitually rather than consciously choose. Because it has become a habit, responding emotionally is much easier than reflecting and consciously choosing:

- It's easy to not pay attention, hard to really listen to others.
- It's easy to judge, hard to accept.
- It's easy to hate, hard to forgive.
- It's easy to communicate passively or aggressively, hard to be assertive.

18

Unfortunately, these unconscious reactions don't often produce what is best for ourselves and others. **Again, no one ever said this was easy. This path is not founded on always feeling comfortable. It's foundation is leading a life where we do what is best for ourselves and others.** If you are in doubt as to whether you are best serving yourself and others, go with the kindest action. This approach also applies to how we treat ourselves.

As you continue reading, you will be presented with responses to life's challenges that you may never have considered. In time, you will naturally and consistently act from a position of wisdom and compassion when facing a specific stressful situation. But it may take a while before you get there. How soon depends on the understanding you have embodied, how much suffering you are willing to endure before changing and an unknown variable called Grace. Grace is simply knowing that behavior changes at the exact moment it is supposed to change. This knowledge provides us with patience and acceptance for ourselves and those who are important to us.

19

HOW DO YOU MAKE YOURSELF MISERABLE EXERCISE

Do the following exercise, then allow yourself one week to complete the home assignment. Reread the chapter as often as necessary.

A.   **MAKE A LIST OF WHAT YOU DO THAT MAKES YOU MISER-ABLE.** For example:

- Eating too much junk food
- Saying negative things about yourself to yourself
- Arguing
- Not asking for what you want
- Not getting enough sleep

B.   **FOR EACH ITEM ON YOUR LIST SUGGEST SOMETHING ELSE THAT YOU COULD DO IN ORDER TO AVOID BECOMING MIS ERABLE.** For example:

- Instead of eating junk food, you could eat fruit

- Instead of feeling bad about yourself, you could help other people

- Instead of arguing, you could allow five uninterrupted minutes for each person to explain their point of view

- Instead of not asking for what you want, you could make a list and move through your passiveness by asking for what you want in the appropriate moment

- Instead of not getting enough sleep, you could turn the TV off at 11 o'clock every evening

YOU ALWAYS HAVE A CHOICE

1. REFLECTING ON YOUR PAST, WRITE DOWN THE MOST SIG-
    NIFICANT CHOICES YOU HAVE MADE IN YOUR LIFE.
    For example: quitting smoking, moving, getting married,
    having kids, etc.

2. CHOOSE ONE ITEM FOR YOUR "HOW DO YOU MAKE YOUR-
    SELF MISERABLE" LIST AND USE THE JOURNAL FORMAT
    BELOW TO RECORD THE RESULTS OF A NEW CHOICE YOU
    MAKE RATHER THAN MAKING YOURSELF MISERABLE.

21

Journal Format

•   Describe the situation

•   How do you usually respond to the situation?

•   List some alternative responses

•   What happened when new responses were used compared to the
    habitual ones?

•   What have you learned?

3. DURING THE WEEK KEEP A DAILY RECORD OF SITUATIONS
    IN WHICH, BY CHOOSING A DIFFERENT RESPONSE FROM
    YOUR HABITUAL ONE, YOU SAW POSITIVE CHANGES. Be
    open to the possibilities that new choices can bring.

PARTICIPANTS' COMMENTS

These comments are included to give you some idea of what other parents, teachers, and students have experienced. When applicable, they can provide valuable insight regarding issues you may be dealing with in your own life. I ask you to be open to the possibilities that new choices can bring.

- A woman shared her emotional pain about being unable to hug or even lovingly touch her 14 year-old daughter. She also realized how much her inability to show affection upset her daughter. She said that she just did not feel natural being affectionate. My suggestion was that she should just reach out and do it even though it didn't feel natural. She tried it and commented: "At first I felt a little phony and unnatural. After reaching out several times, it became a lot easier and I actually started to enjoy being affectionate with my daughter."

- A mother complained that she couldn't stand it when her husband and 13 year-old daughter constantly argued with each other. She would listen for a while, but would inevitably get upset and yell at them both for fighting. The class pointed out that maybe this wasn't her battle and that, maybe, the problem her husband and daughter were having was their problem to work out. When she was asked, "Does your intervention do any good?" she sighed and said, "No." The new choice she shared in her homework was to leave the house and go inline skating whenever their arguing started getting to her. She reported that this choice was really working for her because the frequency of their arguing decreased, since it appears that her husband and daughter missed her presence when she would leave the house.

- A ninth grade English teacher felt miserable because upon arriving home each day after work she was responsible for everything that her three children needed. Her husband would come home from a day's work and read the paper or sit and watch TV. She recalled,

"One day I made the choice to tell him that he was not free to just sit on the couch and read the paper when he came home. I'm lucky that my husband is very understanding and after I spoke up he now assists with taking care of the kids."

- A teacher reported on her mid-term examination, "I always have a choice in how I will handle situations that occur within my class room. For example, if a student seems to be getting disrespectful with me, I have a choice whether to ignore the situation, confront the student in front of everyone or discuss the situation after class. I find it is usually better to discuss the situation after class because it alleviates a lot of pressure for both of us. A student doesn't feel pressured to impress anyone when there is a private one on one discussion. In front of the class, a student feels pressure to look good and the teacher wants to show she has control."

- A wonderful parent stated, "I used to constantly argue with my husband about anything and everything. Over the weeks, I have learned that when he says something that annoys me I can just listen and not argue. At first he didn't know how to act. My lack of response just made him angrier. But recently he has gotten a lot lighter with his requests and conversations with me. I feel better about him and I know he feels better about himself — and me, I hope."

- After working on the destructive habit of saying "yes" when she wanted to say "no," a teacher responded: "Sometimes I feel I may hurt someone's feelings if I say 'no.' When I say 'yes' when I really want to say 'no,' I could kick myself. I get angry with myself and at the person I said 'yes' to. Of course I never tell them or let them know I am angry. Sometimes I feel used, even though I know it was my choice to say 'yes'. After reading the assignment, I decided that if the situation arose again, I would say what I really wanted to say. There were two times last week when something was asked of me where I felt it was expected that I say 'yes'. I told both people 'no'. The result was that I felt better about my choices. I didn't have any turmoil within me about what I should or should not have said. I didn't feel as if I was doing something that I didn't want to do, either."

- "I have a student who I thought had selective memory loss. It seemed the more I explained a set of directions, the more he claimed he didn't know what to do. Consequently, I stopped listening to him. My body language clearly reflected my displeasure with the student. I finally realized that he wanted my attention for himself and this was his way of getting my attention. I now make a conscious effort to give this child more responsibility. For example, having him check papers, calling on him for answers, etc. By choosing to respond to his needs, his attention demanding methods subsided."

- A mother was upset because her eight year old son, a great artist, was the "class clown" who was always seeking approval from his classmates. Another parent suggested, "My son was very much like yours at that age. After several attempts at counseling produced very little resolution, I decided to enroll him in an after school arts program. Almost overnight he became more confident and less needy around his peers." Discovering an effective approach often requires creativity, persistence and the humility to ask others for help.

2

WHO'S REALLY LISTENING?

Focused listening is the essence of communication and the first step to being a masterful educator.

We have all been told that in order to be successful in life, we must learn how to effectively communicate. We take this advice to heart and try very hard to find ways to clearly express our thoughts and feelings, state our opinions, and offer advice. The problem with this approach, however, is that the kind of communication we seek, the real "meeting of the minds" that we want, does not begin with talking — it begins with listening, really listening. Countless hours are spent teaching us how to speak and express ourselves. But how many of us were taught how to really listen so we can understand how others see the world and better respond to their needs.

The importance of listening becomes more profound when we consider that 55 percent of what is communicated occurs through body language, 38 percent with tone of voice and only 7 percent through what is said. In order to listen, really listen, and access all the factual, emotional and psychological information that is available in any communication, we need to quiet our minds. We need to turn off the play-by-play commentator, resist the snap judgments and listen.

QUIET PLEASE

Do you experience a place inside of you that is quiet? A place where there is just silence? Is there a place in your mind were there is no chatter? You do not have to experience this place all or most of the time to answer yes. Let's make it even easier. You can answer "yes" if you just believe that such a place exists. For those of you who have never experienced quietness of mind and think that it can only occur after a lobotomy, I have an exercise for you:

- Read the first paragraph of this chapter again. (I'm trusting you, please don't let me down.)
- Read it another time and note whether you were having any distracting thoughts while you were reading.
- Read the section again and whatever thoughts come to mind, let them go and come back to just reading the material.

Now let's talk about what you just experienced. When you were taking in the information on the page, a part of you was quiet. In these moments when your mind was still, you were just receiving the information—nothing else.

Were you able to experience this quietness? I hope so. You must be quiet inside in order to really focus and pay attention. When you were thinking about what the words meant, judging my instructions or thinking about whether you had paid the phone bill, you were doing something other than focusing on the first paragraph. **It's a matter of choosing where you focus your attention.** Are you focusing on the words on the page or on your thoughts?

I WANT TO BE LIKE MIKE

When basketball superstar Michael Jordan is driving to the hoop and is just about to stuff the ball, do you think he is thinking about how his muscles are working, how fast he's moving, how hard he's breathing, or what's for dinner? Or is he instinctively moving in for the score?

Think about dancing. Doesn't it feel wonderful when the music flows through you and moves your body? What would your dancing look like if your mind chattered, "OK, now raise the left leg two inches, set it down and put weight on it while swinging the right leg three inches?" or "I wonder if I'm doing this right?" Have you ever seen anyone dance awkwardly? This is the result of an active mind participating in an area where it doesn't belong.

Masterful listening requires a quiet, receptive mind. **When you are practicing masterful listening — the kind of listening that can really make a difference — you are simply being receptive to what the other person is saying. Nothing else.** Sometimes parents tell me, "I can wash the dishes, talk on the phone and still listen to my kid." This is not focused, masterful listening. This is washing the dishes, talking on the phone and half-heartedly listening

THE TOP THIRTEEN THINGS WE DO INSTEAD OF REALLY LISTENING

1. We think about a solution to the other person's problem before they have finished.

2. We assume that the other person doesn't know what he is talking about.

3. We space out. Because of boredom, restlessness or our own short attention span we start to think about something completely unrelated.

4. We react to one part of what the other person is saying and interrupt, evaluate, probe or advise.

5. We internally rehearse our response while the other person is still speaking.

6. We worry about what the other person is thinking about us.

7. We become annoyed and impatient with the other person's pace or accent.

8. We do something else while listening.

9. We react defensively to what is said by getting angry or shutting down.

10. We try to identify with the speaker by telling our own story.

11. We try to listen when we are emotionally out of balance or physically exhausted.

12. We judge the person who's speaking. This includes judging people's clothes, appearance or manner, and indulging any prejudice that prevents real listening.

13. We are attached to our own point of view and are not totally open to what is being said.

Course participants are often confused when I suggest to them that offering a solution is not listening. They often say, "Isn't it my job as a teacher to provide guidance?" We're not really listening when we think about a solution at the same time someone is discussing an issue. The result is more beneficial when we listen first, take it all in, and then allow our inner wisdom to come forward with an appropriate response. The process becomes a dance of receiving and responding.

Sometimes, when we share a problem, we're not really looking for a solution — just someone to listen. When you have a problem, you may call a friend just to "talk" — not to get "fixed." Kids are the same way. Often they're not looking for a particular answer. They just want you to listen.

How often have you found yourself trying to reason with your students, presenting them with what you know is a practical solution, only to see it all fall on deaf ears because they have already taken a position and dug in? We often end up in a showdown where an endless argument ensues and the student is forced to do something against his or her will or stomps off in disgust. **Masterful listening can create a safe, loving and caring environment where you can drop rather then defend a position.** Often your student will feel honored and empowered simply because you have taken the time to listen. It is from this empowered position that they can find their own answers.

HOW DEEP CAN LISTENING GO?

When we practice masterful listening we are experiencing more than just hearing the other person's voice. We understand who we are dealing with not only by their words but also by how we feel inside while engaged in the conversation. We actually "feel" and "intuit" the other person's intentions, emotions, needs and fears. The tone, the nuances, the body language and the facial expressions are all ways we come to know this person. The deeper we listen, the more information is available to us and the better we can understand the other person's point of view.

An example of the depth that listening can reach was poignantly demonstrated in a research project. When I use this example, sometimes workshop participants get upset. I hope you understand the spirit of the research and the learning that it reveals.

A mother rabbit was placed on a beach and wired with a heart monitor. Her babies were put on a boat and taken five miles out to sea and sacrificed. At the very moment that the bunnies were killed, the mother's heart rate changed dramatically. Even though they were five miles away, her body sensed what was happening to her babies. This phenomenon can be categorized as listening at a very deep level, a level that involves intuition and feeling. Mothers often report instances of knowing what is happening with their children even though they are not physically with them. **When the mind is quiet, when you are able to stop the chattering, a whole new world of possibilities opens.**

PUTTING MASTERFUL LISTENING INTO PRACTICE

Now, let's put masterful listening into practice. This lesson means very little unless you are willing to do the home assignment. The more committed you are, the more benefits you will receive. So here's another opportunity to live more of your potential.

MASTERFUL LISTENING

Over the next seven days observe what it is like to practice listening to a student and record the specifics of at least one communication per day. A family member, friend or co-worker can be used for this exercise if it is not possible to work with a student. You can also use more than one person. Write down the answers to the following questions (I suggest you use the worksheet that follows the questions):

1. **WHAT DID YOUR STUDENT SAY?** Be brief. Simply record the general topic of conversation; for example: "We spoke about her wanting new shoes" or "She told me about her problems with another teacher." There is no need to give a word-for-word account.

30

2. **DID YOU DO ANYTHING INSTEAD OF LISTENING?** Did you practice masterful listening or were you distracted? Please be honest! If necessary, refer back to the Top Thirteen List.

3. **WHAT EMOTIONS DID YOU EXPERIENCE DURING YOUR C O N - VERSATION?** Be specific. For example: "I experienced anger, boredom, surprise, disappointment, etc."

4. **DID YOU EXPERIENCE YOUR STUDENT OR THE SITUATION IN A DIFFERENT WAY WHEN YOU PRACTICED MASTERFUL LISTENING?** For example: "I thought Johnny was being disrespectful, but I came to realize that he was just confused."

I HAVE ALWAYS HATED HOMEWORK

The top six excuses for not doing the listening homework:

1. I was too busy to practice listening.
2. My student lost his voice.
3. I lost my hearing for a week.
4. My student stayed home from school.
5. I ran away from home.
6. I totally forgot there was homework.

The single biggest reason for doing the listening homework:

Research has shown that we learn and retain:

10% of what we hear

15% of what we see

20% of what we see and hear

40% of what we discuss with others

80% of what we experience directly and practice (i.e. homework)

90% of what we attempt to teach others

TIPS FOR MASTERFUL LISTENING

- Be willing to listen without doing something else at the same time.
- Accept the other person.
- Respect that all human beings are valuable. We may not agree with what they have to say, but they have a right to say what is true for them.
- Acknowledge that every person has the capacity to solve his or her own problems (we don't have to "fix" them).
- Create adequate time to listen.
- Realize that the goal of listening is to understand the other person.

WE TEACH WHO WE ARE — NOT WHAT WE KNOW

LISTENING HOMEWORK WORKSHEET

DAY 1

1. NATURE OF COMMUNICATION:

2. WHAT DID YOU DO INSTEAD OF LISTENING?

33

3. EMOTIONS THAT YOU EXPERIENCED:

4. REALIZATIONS THAT OCCURRED FROM DOING THE EXERCISE:

LISTENING HOMEWORK WORKSHEET

DAY 2

1. NATURE OF COMMUNICATION:

2. WHAT DID YOU DO INSTEAD OF LISTENING?

34

3. EMOTIONS THAT YOU EXPERIENCED:

4. REALIZATIONS THAT OCCURRED FROM DOING THE EXERCISE:

LISTENING HOMEWORK WORKSHEET

DAY 3

1. NATURE OF COMMUNICATION:

2. WHAT DID YOU DO INSTEAD OF LISTENING?

3. EMOTIONS THAT YOU EXPERIENCED:

4. REALIZATIONS THAT OCCURRED FROM DOING THE EXERCISE:

LISTENING HOMEWORK WORKSHEET

DAY 4

1. NATURE OF COMMUNICATION:

2. WHAT DID YOU DO INSTEAD OF LISTENING?

3. EMOTIONS THAT YOU EXPERIENCED:

4. REALIZATIONS THAT OCCURRED FROM DOING THE EXERCISE:

LISTENING HOMEWORK WORKSHEET

DAY 5

1.   NATURE OF COMMUNICATION:

2.   WHAT DID YOU DO INSTEAD OF LISTENING?

37

3.   EMOTIONS THAT YOU EXPERIENCED:

4.   REALIZATIONS THAT OCCURRED FROM DOING THE EXERCISE:

LISTENING HOMEWORK WORKSHEET

DAY 6

1. NATURE OF COMMUNICATION:

2. WHAT DID YOU DO INSTEAD OF LISTENING?

38

3. EMOTIONS THAT YOU EXPERIENCED:

4. REALIZATIONS THAT OCCURRED FROM DOING THE EXERCISE:

LISTENING HOMEWORK WORKSHEET

DAY 7

1. NATURE OF COMMUNICATION:

2. WHAT DID YOU DO INSTEAD OF LISTENING?

39

3. EMOTIONS THAT YOU EXPERIENCED:

4. REALIZATIONS THAT OCCURRED FROM DOING THE EXERCISE:

PARTICIPANTS' COMMENTS

- A mother of a 14-year-old responded, "I never understood what the teachers meant when they said my daughter was so sweet. Last night when I really listened to my daughter and didn't try to interject my 'I-know-better' point of view, I experienced what her teachers were talking about."

- "After the listening class I realized that there was a wise guy student that I was not listening to. Every time he opened his mouth, I pre-judged what he was going to say and basically turned myself off. This week I listened to what he had to say and although there was some silliness, there were also things that he said that were very important to hear."

- I found this fourth grade teacher's "listening" experience to be very profound: "A student explained that she was often late because she doesn't have an alarm clock and her mother wakes her up late. I noticed that while she was speaking I felt upset and at the same time, I was trying to find a solution to her dilemma. I saw for the first time that this is what I normally do — solve a problem rather then use masterful listening.

  "The next day I went up to her and asked her what was wrong. I asked if it was hard for her to get up in the morning and if she went to bed late. She simply stated that she didn't like coming to school because she felt dumb because she had been left back last year. I let her speak and carefully listened which helped me realize that her lateness did not stem from laziness but from insecurities and lack of motivation."

- An eighth grader observed, "When I listened instead of spacing out or wanting to be right, I realized that the reason my mother wanted me to be home by 9:00 was that she cared and was concerned for my safety."

- Another mother said, "In the past, I usually didn't pay much attention to what my eight-year-old daughter had to say. But when I listened to her, she started telling me things about herself that I never knew before. Some of these things weren't pleasant to hear. She told me she felt that I didn't love her as much as I loved her younger sister. I never realized she felt this way and, as a result of her sharing, I was able to tell her that I loved her just as much as I love her sister. I learned that people open up when we give them the space to open up."

- A mother of three reported, "I used to talk and listen to all three kids at once. What I did differently as a result of this listening assignment was take time in a private space and listen to one child at a time. I was amazed at how much each one opened up and how they shared information about themselves that I never knew before."

- Another parent commented, "My husband is telling me about his job. Some of his deals have fallen through. I don't respond. I hear him repeating the same thing over and over. 'I got to make money, I got to make money.' I don't react or question him. What I hear for the first time is his frustration with the rate of progress he's making and his concerns about our upcoming vacation. Today, I'm not angry with him for being preoccupied. I think maybe I understand him more because I listened."

- An educator shared this story: "A fellow teacher came to me asking for advice regarding how to finish her master's degree. I was able to give her my undivided attention as she spoke about how her responsibilities at home, work and school were interfering with her education. As I was listening, she was able to find a way to schedule her time so she could complete her schooling. She thanked me for just listening."

Masterful listening is not something that you do only with your students. As you practice listening and become more and more aware of what you do instead of listening, you will find that this skill applies to every relationship in your life. What you do instead of listening may depend on whether you are communicating with your child, spouse or a work colleague but I promise you, if you become a better listener, your relationships will improve.

42

3

TAKE CARE OF YOURSELF SO YOU CAN HELP TAKE CARE OF OTHERS

Being a Masterful Teacher requires the ability to take care of ourselves so we can better nurture our students.

In our desire to be good teachers, it's easy to forget to take care of ourselves. Between making sure our lesson plans are complete, grades are in, after school commitments are met and taking care of our own home, it seems almost impossible to find any time for ourselves.

When we become teachers, we do not stop being human beings—people with needs that must be acknowledged. To be balanced and whole, we need time to reflect, relax and experience peace. We all have experienced the difference in teaching effectiveness when we are well rested and prepared compared to being frazzled and pressured. We need to take care of ourselves so we can better take care of others.

PRACTICAL WAYS OF TAKING CARE OF YOURSELF

To take better care of ourselves, we need to be nurtured on four basic levels: the physical, the emotional, the mental and the spiritual.

On a **physical** level, if we become ill or rundown it is difficult to function effectively. Regular exercise, sound nutrition and adequate rest positively influence our quality of life on every level.

On an **emotional** level, if we are upset about something that happens at work or with our spouse or a friend and we don't deal with it appropriately, the discord often spills over into our interaction with our students. Relationships thrive when we accept, understand and effectively communicate our feelings.

On a **mental** level, boredom, routine and lack of stimulation produce frustration and rob us of vitality. Reading, expanding our professional knowledge, being with interesting people and learning new things are important ways to enrich our lives.

On a **spiritual** level, if we feel lost, hopeless and in despair, it becomes difficult for our children to be inspired. Trust in ones own worth and the basic goodness of life opens the door to Grace.

The following are ways we can better take care of ourselves:

PHYSICAL

Exercising

Eating better

Relaxing

Meditating

Sharing some of the responsibility for the care of our children with family members or other trusted people

Getting our hair done; having a manicure

Taking a vacation

Taking time for an enjoyable hobby or craft

EMOTIONAL

Calling a friend just to talk about what's going on in your life

Expressing needs

Listening to music

Giving and receiving affection (animals count!)

Having a social life

MENTAL

Taking courses

Reading a book

Exploring an idea for a project

Following up on plans for further education

Reading and completing the exercises in this book

SPIRITUAL

Taking time out for prayer, meditation or other religious practices

Making a commitment to personal growth

Writing in a journal

Reading material from spiritual teachers

Sending positive thoughts to someone who is ill or unhappy

Spending time with uplifting people

Helping others

Practicing humility, gratitude and compassion

Many of these suggestions have benefits on more than one level. For instance, after exercising, we not only feel better physically, but are often more balanced emotionally and mentally as well. Another example would be the way in which the foods we eat can affect our state of mind. Time and time again I have observed that certain foods have a negative effect on my emotional well being. I always think, "This time it will be different." But sure enough, almost every time after eating sugar I become mentally unfocused or seem to get upset by a circumstance that usually wouldn't upset me. For many of us, the foods that have the greatest likelihood of producing an allergic reaction are: sugar, wheat, dairy and soy products.

Likewise, when we meditate we feel mentally alert, physically renewed and emotionally calmed as well as spiritually uplifted. During meditation we stop for a period of time and observe rather than getting carried away by the moment-to-moment activity of our mind, emotions and body. We slow down and become aware of the ongoing, habitual and unproductive nature of most of our thoughts. Also, as a result of meditation, we tend to more naturally make choices that serve ourselves and others. It's as if we don't have to think about the right thing to do. Meditation places us directly in the flow of what is appropriate for everyone. **The social and emotional educational methods presented in this book, coupled with meditation and exercise, are very powerful tools in changing habitual patterns of thought and behavior that do not serve us.**

THE IMPORTANCE OF RELAXATION

Everybody has a different way of nurturing and taking care of themselves. One of the most effective and often neglected ways of nurturing ourselves involves periodic relaxation. Listen to this mother of six: "For years, from the moment I woke up to get my kids ready for school till I went to bed after midnight, I took no time to relax. Then, about a year ago, I decided that my parenting would improve if I first took better care of myself. So every day, no matter what, I locked myself in the bathroom for a minimum of 20 minutes to take a relaxing bath. Instead of being frazzled, I became recharged and able to more effectively deal with the kids."

KIDS ALSO DESERVE A BREAK TODAY

Children are confronted with the realities of AIDS, weapons possession, suicide, violence in the media, terrorism, and drug and alcohol abuse — challenges few of us encountered when we were growing up. A study assessing the emotional well-being of seven - to fourteen-year-old American children emphatically illustrates this observation. Done first in the mid-1970s, then repeated with similar youth 15 years later, the survey found that, on average, the basic indicators of emotional health for America's children had declined across the board. They were more impulsive, disobedient, anxious, fearful, lonely and sad. Childrens' scores declined on 42 such indicators and improved on none of them over the 15-year period. There were also significant increases in the frequency of teen violence, suicide, rape and the number of weapons-related crimes.

We need to demonstrate more empathy for children. We can nurture them by encouraging them to engage in stress-reducing activities such as physical recreation and relaxation. Many of the other suggestions mentioned for taking care of ourselves can also be applied to our students.

46

"NOBODY IS GOING TO GIVE YOU WHAT YOU DON'T THINK YOU DESERVE"

In class, I often quote sayings and share stories that were told to me by teachers. But one time, an original, honest-to-goodness quote came out of my mouth: "Nobody is going to give you what you don't think you deserve." I've been thinking more and more deeply about this ever since I first said it. I believe that at a deep level we have created our present financial situation, relationships and life-styles because they are what we think we deserve. Let me give you an example: I asked my class of senior high school students, "How much money would you like to make once you are established in the world?" One student responded, "Forty-five thousand dollars a year." Another student said, "Two-hundred and fifty thousand dollars a year." I asked the second student what his father did. "My father is part owner of the King Ranch," he said, "on the island of Hawaii."

Having lived in Hawaii, I knew that the King Ranch was not only the largest ranch there, but in the entire United States as well. For this student, $250,000 was not a lot of money, whereas $45,000 was a lot of money for the first student. These two students were similar ethically and academically. It was their different socioeconomic backgrounds that influenced their financial expectations. When we begin taking total responsibility for what we think we deserve, we can begin the process of functioning on a more fulfilling level physically, emotionally, mentally and spiritually. This process of change begins with looking at the source of the beliefs we have about our capacity or our right to manifest our full potential at every level. This can lead to a profound consideration of the limitless possibilities that are available to us as human beings, leading to meaningful actions that bring these possibilities into reality. This idea was beautifully expressed in Nelson Mandela's 1994 Inaugural Address where he quoted a statement attributed to Marianne Williamson:

"Our worst fear is not that we are inadequate. Our deepest fear is that we are powerful beyond measure. It is our light not our darkness that most frightens us. We ask ourselves, who am I to be brilliant, gorgeous, talented and fabulous? Actually, who are you not to be? You are a child of God. Your playing small doesn't serve the world. There is nothing enlightened about shrinking so that others don't feel insecure around you. We were born to make manifest the glory of God within us. It is in everyone and as we let our own light shine we unconsciously give other people permission to do the same. As we are liberated from our fear our presence automatically liberates others."

48

TAKING CARE OF YOURSELF

1. EVERY DAY FOR THE NEXT WEEK, DO SOMETHING NICE FOR YOURSELF (ON A PHYSICAL, EMOTIONAL, MENTAL OR SPIRITUAL LEVEL) THAT YOU DON'T USUALLY DO. Make it simple and practical so you can complete the exercise. For instance, it may be more realistic for you to walk for ten minutes each day rather than running three miles.

2. EVERY DAY FOR THE NEXT WEEK, FREEFORM WRITE AT LEAST TWO PAGES (FRONT AND BACK SIDE IS ONE PAGE). Freeform writing is a technique that enables you to let go of emotional and mental tension. Sit in a quiet area and write down whatever comes to your mind. Just write down whatever you are thinking without changing it in any way. For example: "I'm bored, tired, cooking, noise sound what are they up to?" The whole exercise usually takes about ten minutes. After this is completed, it is important that you do not reread what you wrote, but instead rip up the paper, burn it or flush it away. This can be a very powerful exercise. I receive the most benefit from this exercise when I do it first thing in the morning or after a stressful day.

49

3. EACH DAY, ACKNOWLEDGE TO YOURSELF THAT YOU ARE A GOOD TEACHER, DOING THE BEST YOU CAN AND THAT YOU HAVE YOUR STUDENT'S BEST INTEREST AT HEART. You might want to list the specific reasons you are a good teacher. (For example, you take time preparing lessons, you are compassionate, you spend time with individual students when necessary etc.) It sounds simple, but just try it!

4. IF YOU HAVE THE RELAXATION TAPE, THIS IS A GOOD TIME TO BEGIN LISTENING TO IT.

PARTICIPANTS' COMMENTS

- One mother responded, "Last week was the first time in years that I went out and had lunch by myself. It might not sound like a big deal but when you eat practically every meal with your two young sons, it really is a pleasure to enjoy a quiet meal alone."

- Another mother said, "I followed your suggestion and twice last week I locked myself in the bathroom and took a 20 minute bubble bath. At one point my six-year-old started banging on the door and I explained to him that this was my 'time out' and that I would play with him when I was done. After a minute or two of crying, he went into his room and occupied himself."

- A teacher shared, "I used to routinely eat the school lunches and I noticed that after lunch I was tired and irritable. I decided to bring salads and home cooked food each day for lunch. I was delighted to see that my energy level does not drop anymore after eating."

- Another mother responded, "I really did something different. Six years ago, before we had our daughter, my husband and I used to love to go out dancing. Last Saturday night we splurged. We got a babysitter and went out to a club and danced until two in the morning."

- A mother of three shared, "I haven't exercised there yet, but last Tuesday I joined a health club."

- A teacher responded, "The thing that usually makes me the most miserable is my weight. Growing up, I was always thin but after giving birth to my third child, it has been very difficult to take off the extra seven to ten pounds. I sometimes deal with this in a negative way by eating anything I want because I say to myself, 'What difference does it make if I am overweight?' I have begun to deal with it in a positive way by watching what I eat and exercising four times a week."

4

REFLECTION BEFORE ACTION— HOW YOU RELATE TO THE ISSUE IS THE ISSUE

The development of reflection and considering the consequences before taking action not only transforms behavior, but also is the true source of self-knowledge, creativity and self-esteem.

In my workshops I ask my students, "You're driving down the street and someone cuts you off. What choices do you have?"

Typical responses include: "I'd yell at them..." "I'd swear under my breath..." "I'd cut them off..." "Ignore them and just drive on..."

Now I ask, "What are the consequences of each of these responses?" (You can answer this for yourself.)

One day, while walking on 14th Street in New York City, I saw a man driving a convertible sports car with a woman seated next to him. Behind him were two men in a SUV. The men in the SUV had beeped the horn a couple of times to encourage the man in the sports car to speed up. When they stopped at a light, the man driving the sports car grabbed his Club locking device, walked over to the SUV and smashed every window in their vehicle (I know many of you think this is a typical occurrence in New York City, but, trust me, it isn't). Think about the consequences of this response on all the concerned parties.

Along the same lines, I'll ask my teenage students, "You sit down in the cafeteria. Unexpectedly, you see that you're right next to someone you know has been talking about you behind your back. What do you do?"

The usual responses include: "I'd hit him..." "I'd yell at him..." "I'd ignore him..." "I'd talk to him and see if it is true..." "I'd move my seat..."

Then I ask, "What are the consequences of each of these responses?"

This is the important question each of us needs to continuously ask ourselves throughout the day.

OF MICE AND MEN

Years ago, a teacher of mine told me a wonderful story that relates to reflection and action:

"You know, people are just like rats. The only difference is that rats are smarter. Let me give you an example. You take a piece of cheese and put it at the end of a maze. You take a rat and put him behind a gate at the beginning of the maze. When you open the gate, the rat will go through the maze, eat the cheese and return to where he started. Every time you open the gate, the same course of events occurs: the rat goes through the maze, eats cheese and returns. The fifth time you open the gate, you take away the cheese. The rat goes through the maze, finds no cheese and returns. You open the gate and again take away the cheese. The rat will again negotiate the maze, find no cheese and return. The third time you provide no cheese and open the gate, however, the rat will just stand there and not bother to go through the maze. Rats are like people. The only difference is that rats are smarter. The rat knows to stop a certain behavior when there is no cheese. Humans keep doing the same thing over and over and over, expecting cheese long after they should have realized that there is no cheese to be had."

How many times have we eaten food that over and over has made us feel bad and convinced ourselves that this time it would be different? Or instead of something you have eaten, how about something that's eating you? How about a relationship that just doesn't work? Have you noticed how we often pick the same person (but with a different name and shoe size) as the one that made us miserable, expecting that "this one will be different"? **To expect different results from the same actions or series of actions is crazy.**

HOW YOU RELATE TO THE ISSUE IS THE ISSUE

A woman has just cooked breakfast for her husband (reverse the gender roles if you like). After eating, he walks out the door saying, "See ya later."

She shouts after him, "See ya later? What do you mean, see ya later? Every day I cook for you. I get up every morning and make the coffee, toast the bread, scramble the eggs, set the table, clean up and wash the dishes after you leave — and all you can say is, 'See ya later'?"

He responds, "There'd be no food to cook if I didn't go to work every day while you just stay home."

"Oh yeah?" she responds, "You try it! You see how easy it is staying home with these kids everyday!"

We'll leave the rest of the discussion to your imagination. Now the apparent issue here is that two people have just had a fight and have gone off angry at each other. **But the real issue is not the fight — it's how they're going to relate to the fight.** Let's look at positive and negative choices people make when relating to issues. Negative ways include: worrying, sleeping, denial, getting even, violence, eating, smoking, drugs, alcohol, and staring at the TV. Many people use negative habits in order to avoid dealing with life's problems.

Positive ways of dealing with being upset include relaxing, taking a hot bath, reading, enjoying a hobby, crying, meditating, talking to a friend or counselor, exercising, and discussing the problem with the appropriate person. Positive solutions usually incorporate aspects of acceptance, communication, forgiveness, self respect and respect for others.

The quality of our life changes when we take time to reflect and make positive choices that lift ourselves and others out of pain and into healing.

Inevitably, whenever we discuss How You Relate to the Issue is the Issue, the topic of worrying comes up. When used constructively, worrying motivates us to take appropriate action. For instance, your 12-year-old daughter says she'll return from a friend's house by 5:00p.m. It's now 5:30 and you begin to worry. After a short while you call the friend's house in order to find out your daughter's whereabouts. At its best, worrying is a call to action.

In contrast, let's say you have an important job interview coming up in two days. You observe that you are beginning to worry incessantly. You know that you have taken every step you could to be prepared for the interview, e.g. picked out the right clothes, found out as much as you could about the company, arranged for transportation, etc. At this point, because there is nothing left to do, worrying only serves to make you miserable.

Class members often protest, "It's only because I care that I worry. If I didn't care, I wouldn't even think of worrying." My experience is that when we care there are other positive choices available to us. After the appropriate action is taken, does the act of worrying do anything for you or the other person besides making you sick?

Let me reinforce this notion with another example: When I ask a group of parents, "What do you worry about?" frequently I get the response, "I worry about my child's safety going to and from school."

Your child is walking home after school and you are sitting home worrying. Are you making your child safer by worrying? Are you doing anything to help your child by worrying? I suspect the answer to both of these questions is "no". The issue is your child's safety on the way home from school. So I ask, "What constructive action could you take in this situation?" (I did have several parents say that instead of worrying they drive their child to and from school each day. This is a great solution but inappropriate or impractical for most of us.)

Another possibility we came up with in class was to picture your child surrounded by God's protective light, with a smile on her face, safely walking home from school. Does this choice hurt you? Does this choice hurt your child? At worst, it doesn't hurt her, and at best it may help her. Remember the rabbits from earlier on? Energy can be projected out from beyond our bodies and affect others. Many parents have reported that this choice works a lot better than worrying.

Before doing the following home assignment, I would like to mention one more helpful observation regarding the nature of worrying. Many of us want to control the way things are. **Worrying is an expression of the fear that comes from not being in control of a situation.**

From early infancy we teach children values and what we believe to be the correct way to respond to life's challenges. There comes a point when children know what we expect of them. Still, they are going to do what they are going to do. Worrying represents the fear that what they are going to do is what we don't want them to do. **In reality, when a 15 year-old walks out the door, we have no control over him or her.**

55

HOW YOU RELATE TO THE ISSUE IS THE ISSUE

1. TO BETTER UNDERSTAND THE REAL NATURE OF WORRY AND ITS FUTILITY, SIT DOWN FOR TEN MINUTES AND DO NOTHING ELSE BUT WORRY ABOUT WHAT YOU USUALLY WORRY ABOUT. Could you last the full ten minutes? Now for the rest of the day, don't dwell on any worrying thoughts that enter your mind. Instead make an agreement with yourself to dwell on these thoughts in your next ten minute worrying session. Repeat this exercise each day for one week.

2. PICK ONE AREA OF YOUR LIFE THAT YOU TEND TO WORRY ABOUT HABITUALLY. Use the journal format below to explore different choices you could make regarding how you relate to this area of your life. Take the appropriate action and note the results.

JOURNAL WRITING

A. Describe the situation

B. What is your usual response?

C. What alternative choice or choices did you consider?

D. What were the consequences of your new choices compared with the results of your usual responses?

E. What did you learn? What insight did you gain from this exercise?

PARTICIPANTS' COMMENTS

- A middle school teacher spoke of the change that occurred when she viewed a situation differently. "My class never reached 100 percent school uniform compliance because of one particular student. I became upset with him and so did the rest of the class. I calmed down and took the student out of the room and speak to him about not wearing his uniform. He became upset because his parents did not have the money to purchase a uniform. We spoke to the principal about the situation. We were able to get previously donated uniforms for this student. I had made the mistake of assuming the student did not want to wear his uniform. I was able to correct my misconceptions and find a positive solution."

- Another participant shared, "When my friend died, I created a lot of problems for myself. I blamed his death for my misery and drastic personality and lifestyle changes. Now I realize that it wasn't really his death that caused this — rather, it was how I chose to deal with the loss. If I would have accepted help from those who really cared about me instead of pushing people away and fooling myself into thinking that my actions were really helping my situation, I probably could have avoided wasting so much time hurting myself."

- A man who was participating in my course for drug counselors related an interesting story that is relevant to this particular homework assignment. He told us his reasons for devoting his life to working with drug addicts: "I was a drug addict myself and had expertise in that I was able to kick the habit. Secondly, because of my addiction, I was a waste to society. Becoming a counselor is a way to pay back my debt to society." His tone conveyed that becoming a drug counselor was his punishment for being a drug addict.

  Another drug counselor who had also been a drug addict responded, "Because I was an addict myself, I look at this job as a drug counselor as a gift from God. To be able to now help others is a blessing."

Two drug counselors relating in very different ways to the same issue of being ex-addicts and counselors.

- A mother was very upset because her 12-year-old daughter, who used to hold the mother's hand in public, would no longer spend time with her outside their home. "It's not a warm feeling to know that the child you have nurtured since birth is embarrassed to be seen with you."

  I explained that this is a stage of independence that many adolescents go through and that most adolescents don't want their parents within ten blocks of them when their friends are around. As a result of our discussion, she saw that there were responses to her daughter's behavior other than feeling hurt, resentful and unappreciated. She had more empathy for her daughter when she realized that her daughter was going through a developmental stage that she did not have to take personally.

58

5

ACCEPTANCE

Profound changes occur when we practice acceptance of ourselves, others and the world we live in.

We have spent the first four chapters of this book discussing choices and changes we can make in order to create more fulfilling lives for ourselves and those we care about. But a necessary step in order for change to occur, is to first observe, acknowledge and accept our reality in the present moment. Most of our suffering is a direct result of the programming inside of us that places demands on the world. **In other words, we suffer because we expect circumstances, ourselves and other people to be different from the way they are. In order for change to occur, we must first move from viewing reality as we think it should be to accepting the way it really is.** I'd like to share with you an example from my own life that exemplifies this point.

My mother is 86 years old, widowed and lives in Florida. In one year she moved out of three different residences. Each time her complaint was that the people were too old, too debilitated or not sophisticated enough. I have actually heard her say as others whizzed by while she crept along with assistance from a walker, "There is no way I can stay here. These people are so old and feeble." For years I angrily tried to tell her that her negative perceptions of others were a reflection of her unhappiness. She wouldn't hear it. After repeated moves, I realized she never grasped the meaning of the saying, "Wherever you go, there you are." She seemed to forget that wherever she went, she took herself (and her problems and perceptions) along with her.

One day I realized that my mother's pattern would always be exactly the same — she would behave the same way when she woke up tomorrow and the day after that. The chance of her changing was practically zero. I acknowledged that instead of fighting and judging her I could choose to accept that this is the way she is and that she most likely would never change. This realization was a turning point for me. My relationship with her dramatically improved when I moved from judgment and resentment to acceptance and empathy.

Another instance of accepting people the way they are rather than how we think they should be was exemplified by a student who spoke about her absent father: "My father is a deadbeat liar. But I feel that I am on my way to accepting him for what he is. Before this class I had certain expectations of who my father was supposed to be. It would have been nice if he was the person I wanted him to be. Now I accept who he is and doubt if anybody will fulfill all of my expectations."

Accepting that someone is the way they are does not mean that we like or approve of particular aspects of their personality. Acceptance means allowing a person to be the way they are without expecting them to be different.

60

THE WORD "SHOULD" IS NO GOOD

The story a friend shared with me about his experience of driving to and from the beach each weekend illustrates the power acceptance has to transform our lives.

Tom would leave the city early Friday afternoon in order to avoid the weekend traffic and would return with all the other weekenders Sunday night. The trip that took two hours going would usually take five coming back. His pattern for years was to sit in his car and get really upset. One Sunday, while inching along in his habitually angry state, he noticed that the driver of the car next to his was joyously singing along with the music from his car radio. It finally hit him, "Both of us are going to get home at the same time but he's having a good time and I'm suffering." From that moment on his trip back to the city became a totally different experience. The only thing that had changed was his attitude. He couldn't control the traffic but he could stop demanding that it be different from the way it was.

If we reflect on the previous examples, we can see that my mother, the student's father and the traffic are the way they are and probably will not be any different tomorrow. The same observation applies to most people and events in our lives. **We have a choice of accepting people and occurrences the way they are or fighting reality by saying that they "should" be different. The consequence of the first choice is freedom, peace and compassion; the second choice produces conflict, unhappiness and negativity.**

WHO'S THIS STRANGER LIVING IN MY HOUSE?

Let's look at how the "shoulds" negatively influence the harmony and compassion we share with our teenage students. Adolescence is a time for freedom and individual expression. It's a developmental stage similar to walking at one and talking at two. At the same time they're craving independence, teenagers still have to rely on their parents for shelter, food, clothing, and money. Behavior such as wearing pants around the knees or painting their nails black are often the only ways for many of them to express their individuality and freedom in an environment where they really have very little power. I encourage you to be tolerant and accept their mode of expression for what it is. By not taking their expression so personally, you can avoid difficult and unnecessary power struggles. This does not imply that anything goes — children need boundaries. However, a little tolerance when a teen is testing his or her independence with what are really harmless forms of expression can go a long way toward promoting peace and minimizing more extreme forms of rebellion.

We undermine our relationship with children when we think they "should" do something other than express their feelings. Many of us have grown up in the American culture of "doing". We place a great deal of emphasis on how well we "do" anything. We often approach emotions in the same way. When a child is sad, frustrated, angry or impatient we try to "do" something in order to "fix" the situation and make it better. In reality we must "do" something because we can't bear to just stand by and let children go through the experience of "feeling". Allowing them to experience their emotions can make us feel inadequate, guilty, helpless and out of control. **Underlying this need to "fix" children is our desire to stop their annoying or painful (to us) emotions so we can feel better about ourselves.**

We react this way because most of us learned at an early age that certain emotions are not acceptable. For instance crying, sadness or whining could not be tolerated but had to be "fixed". As a result of generations of parents and teachers reacting to emotions in this manner we have become a society that can't accept feelings. **It has become the cultural norm to use drugs, alcohol, food and cigarettes to dull, dilute and annihilate feelings.**

A more beneficial approach would be to accept our own as well as children's feelings. Loving acceptance of a child's (as well as our own) anger, frustration, impatience and whining is probably the most challenging path we can choose. There are many paths to choose from but, in my experience, acceptance is a more compassionate and rewarding choice than denying or "fixing" emotions that we have labeled as negative.

62

I'M LOOKING AT THE MAN IN THE MIRROR EXERCISE

Often those traits that we have trouble accepting in others are the same ones that we judge as negative in ourselves. As you do the following exercise, you may find that the specific emotions that you don't tolerate in children are the same ones that you don't accept in yourself. These may also be the same emotions that you were forbidden to express as a child.

1. WHICH OF THE EMOTIONAL EXPRESSIONS OF A CHILD ARE DIFFICULT FOR YOU TO ACCEPT? (Examples are: anger, whining, impatience, frustration, loudness, neediness, crying, etc.)

2. WHICH OF YOUR OWN FEELINGS DO YOU HAVE A PROBLEM ACCEPTING?

3. WHEN YOU WERE A CHILD, WHICH FEELINGS WERE YOU NOT ALLOWED TO EXPRESS?

Chastising others for behavior that we judge as negative about ourselves has become one of our favorite pastimes. The critic inside of us who judges the manners, appearance, level of integrity and kindness of others is the same one who gives us a hard time for being ill-mannered, too fat, dishonest, or uncaring. I have been biased against people who are overweight. It is no coincidence that I was teased and that I hated myself for being severely overweight between the ages of eight and twelve. I have very little tolerance for people who smoke cigarettes. Again, I was very hard on myself for two years before I finally stopped smoking.

For many of us, this internal judge and jury goes on non-stop day in and day out. It's no wonder that we get upset, feel alienated and run out of energy. Our life dramatically changes in those moments when we suspend this internal negative dialogue and instead accept people, ourselves and reality it is.

"I FIND IT EASY TO ACCEPT OTHERS BUT WHEN IT COMES TO ACCEPTING MYSELF, IT'S A WHOLE OTHER STORY"

Many of us have no problem accepting others but when it comes to accepting ourselves it's another story. A colleague of mine once used the analogy of the immune system in discussing the process of self-acceptance. The immune system identifies cells as either "self" or "non self." Once it recognizes a cell as "non self," it targets it for destruction. In the same way, every time we have a thought or emotion that we do not accept, the mind in essence is categorizing it as "non self." In doing this, it is attempting to destroy a part of us that is indeed "self." As we noted in the first chapter, this destructive thought pattern is a major cause of dysfunction or disease. This process applies to anger, lust, jealousy and all the other emotions and thoughts we tend to judge as negative and don't accept as parts of who we are.

I once dated a woman for several months before she told me that she smoked. She said that she hated this part of herself and that she was always afraid that someone would reject her when they found out she smoked. I inquired, "Do you judge yourself negatively while you are smoking a cigarette?" "Yes," she replied. I said, "I think it's a wiser choice to enjoy every puff of that cigarette as long as you are going to smoke. In fact, the non-acceptance and guilt you are experiencing may be as injurious to your health as the cigarette itself."

Along the same lines a teacher reported, "Like a chameleon, I was always constantly changing in order to fit in and please those around me. However, once I got in touch with my true self I was able, finally, to love who God loved, and see who God saw. I saw myself as imperfect and human, as I was intended to be. As a result of this revelation I am now able to forgive and accept others in their humanity on a daily basis."

Some people believe that they must be hard on themselves in order to grow, or that acceptance and change are mutually exclusive. Question number 6 in the Home Assignment asks you to address the acceptance issue in a very profound way by observing the part of you that is hard on yourself. **Accepting who we are in each moment does not mean that we will never change. On the contrary, this is the first step necessary for real change to occur.**

ACCEPTANCE

Note: The relatives in this exercise do not need to be living.

1. WHICH OF YOUR MOTHER'S SPECIFIC BEHAVIOR AND PER-
SONALITY TRAITS COULD YOU ACCEPT IN ORDER TO
IMPROVE YOUR RELATIONSHIP WITH HER AND MAKE
YOUR LIFE MORE ENJOYABLE?

2. WHICH OF YOUR FATHER'S SPECIFIC BEHAVIOR AND PER-
SONALITY TRAITS COULD YOU ACCEPT IN ORDER TO
IMPROVE YOUR RELATIONSHIP WITH HIM AND MAKE
YOUR LIFE MORE ENJOYABLE?

3. WHICH OF YOUR SIGNIFICANT OTHER'S SPECIFIC BEHAV-
IOR AND PERSONALITY TRAITS COULD YOU ACCEPT IN
ORDER TO IMPROVE YOUR RELATIONSHIP WITH HIM OR
HER AND MAKE YOUR LIFE MORE ENJOYABLE?

4. WHICH OF YOUR STUDENTS' SPECIFIC BEHAVIOR AND PERSONALITY TRAITS COULD YOU ACCEPT IN ORDER TO IMPROVE YOUR RELATIONSHIP WITH THEM AND MAKE YOUR LIFE MORE ENJOYABLE?

5. WHICH SPECIFIC BEHAVIOR AND PERSONALITY TRAITS OF YOUR OWN COULD YOU ACCEPT INSTEAD OF JUDGING AS NEGATIVE?

6. FOR ONE HOUR EACH DAY, TRY TO ACCEPT YOUR EVERY THOUGHT, EMOTION AND ACTION. FIRST OBSERVE, THEN DISMISS THE PART OF YOU THAT NEGATIVELY JUDGES YOUR THOUGHTS, ACTIONS AND EMOTIONS.

The Serenity Prayer: "God grant me the serenity to accept the things I cannot change, the courage to change the things I can and the wisdom to know the difference."

PARTICIPANTS' COMMENTS

Strong emotions surface whenever we work on resolving issues with people who are very close to us — especially our parents. Be kind to yourself and your parents.

- A parent responded, "One of the things I have had to accept in my 20-year relationship with my husband is that because I am ready to discuss something, even if I think it is important, doesn't mean that he is ready to hear it."

- A teacher shared, "It used to bother me that my pre-K parents look for any excuse to avoid going on trips or attending parent-teacher conferences. I have begun to understand that I will not get as upset if I accept them as they are. If I force them to do things just to please me, none of us will be satisfied. When I accept them and the situation, I feel much better."

67

- Another teacher commented, "I need to accept the fact that my students, as second language learners, are faced with some unique challenges that directly affect their academic progress. Because their parents cannot help with homework, these students are at a disadvantage in a global economy. My students are required to work much harder than many public school children do elsewhere because they need to look outside the home for help with their schoolwork... I need to stop being angry at the world for the plight of the students I teach. In order to be more proactive, I need to put that energy into finding alternatives to help students achieve both in and out of school. I also need to accept that I can only do so much to help the 32 children in my class and that sometimes all that I do will just not be enough."

- A teacher who had recently come from the South shared her feelings of disillusionment about how incredibly different students were in the North compared to the South: "I can't believe the level of disrespect. Children never would think of talking to teachers in the manner that kids do up here. I can't stand being here.

It was obvious that her frustration and pain were mostly caused by her comparison of students from two different locations. She had a big 'should' regarding how students were supposed to be. She came to realize that her way of looking at the issue was not working and that it would be a better choice to start from the point of accepting that these were the students that she was dealing with now, and that they were indeed different from the students that she taught in the South.

- A parent developed a pattern with her sick, cancer-ridden mother. She would tell her about alternative therapies and condemned her for not wanting to try them. This approach consistently created arguments and stress. As part of her acceptance homework she wrote: "I finally realized that our conflict was rooted in my inability to accept that my mother did not believe in alternative therapies. Instead of giving her advice, I told my mother how much I loved and cared for her. This dramatically changed our level of interaction." (Sounds like a great alternative therapy to me!)

- After doing this homework, a woman shared, "I am 32 years old and my mother lives with me. If I'm wearing a dress that is in the least bit revealing when I leave the house, I have to put a sweater over it or my mother will get upset."

"Is there any chance your mother will change?" I asked her.

"No," she replied, " I've tried to talk to her and remind her that I'm 32 years old and it is my house she is living in. This discussion never did any good. Now I just accept that this is the way she is and I take my sweater off as soon as I get outside."

(Note: This is the same strategy that teenagers often use with their parents.)

- A teacher told us that before understanding the principle of acceptance she constantly put herself down for working and not spending enough time with her daughter. In her homework she responded, "I used to be real hard on myself for not spending enough time with my daughter. I have to accept the fact that it is a necessity for me to work and the consequence is that I cannot spend as much time as I would like with my daughter. When I accept this reality and don't judge myself as a bad mother, my daughter seems to be more understanding."

- When asked, "What do you need to accept about your father?" one woman said, "I used to idolize my father and look at him as if he had no faults at all. No man could ever live up to my expectations and as a result, I have yet to have a successful relationship with a man. I now see this pattern clearly. I am also seeing that my father does have faults and that he is a human being like everyone else. This has allowed me to be more realistic in my expectations of men."

- A parent complained that her mother gives card parties at her house several times a week and cooks for everyone. She feels her mother was being taken advantage of because no one else offers to prepare any food. "Do you think your mother enjoys cooking for these people?" I asked her. "Yes," she responded. "Well, you might want to accept the fact that giving to others makes your mother happy."

- A mother stated, "I find myself being disappointed by people all the time. My husband is always late but every time he tells me he'll meet me somewhere at a certain time, I always believe him. My boss at work has lied to me several times, yet whenever she tells me something I always believe her and inevitably I am disappointed."

    Her suffering was the result of viewing people from the vantage point of how she wanted them to be rather than how they really were. She was unwilling to accept the fact that people don't always tell the truth.

- In an ongoing personal growth course I recently attended, Robert stood up and shared how he became upset every time Anthony spoke. He said that he found Anthony to be inauthentic in his expression and he cringed each time Anthony opened his mouth. This was very interesting because each time Robert spoke he was unable to be "real" in his expression. It was obvious to me that Robert was negatively judging Anthony for the same characteristics he possessed.

- A teacher wrote about her experience, "Prior to enrolling in this course, I was of the opinion that acceptance meant agreement. It was quite a revelation to learn that acceptance of a person's negative behavior is a mere acknowledgment of who the individual is, but not necessarily a condoning of those traits. I eventually accepted the fact that a particularly difficult student of mine was a troubled child with very littler or no structure. By accepting him, I was better able to discipline him in a sincere, loving manner."

- A teacher's response clearly exemplified the intention of question 6:

  "I found myself wanting to avoid the assignment because I had no desire to feel anything negative or to feel good about negative thoughts. I began to realize that the thought was not necessarily what caused the discomfort. It was the negative judgment that I had about the thought that made me feel uneasy. I realized that I am very judgmental of myself and that little room is allowed for error. Whenever an error is made I beat myself up before anyone else can.

  "After allowing myself to go through the process several times, one question came to mind, 'How real am I if I only allow myself to look at and accept nice, kind, gentle, sweet thoughts but do not allow myself to look at and see that there are things about me that I may not be totally content with?' I am no less a person if I do not react to a situation the way I felt I should have."

6

RESPONSIBILITY
WHO IS CONTROLLING YOUR LIFE?

*Being responsible begins with viewing each situation from the perspective of how
we created, promoted or allowed what is present.*

We live in a society that often seems to reward a victim mentality. On
daytime talk shows I often observe someone ranting about how they
were "done in" by someone else. Although I have empathy, I still want to
ask, "What part did you play? How did you create, promote or allow this
to happen?" This is what we mean by taking responsibility for what happens in our lives.

Ask yourself this question: "When was I a victim?" Think about a
time when you were picked on, treated unfairly or blamed for something
that wasn't your fault. A ninth grade student's recent response was an
attempt to justify her victimization: "This girl was mad at some of us and
we were just standing there when she hit me. I didn't say anything to
her." "Had you spoken negatively about her behind her back?" I asked.
In answering "yes," she saw how subtle and profound taking responsibility could be. **Taking responsibility is not about being right or wrong.
It's about looking at what part we play in creating, promoting or allowing what happens in our lives.**

A single mother spoke angrily about the "dog" that left her.

I asked her, "Who chose that dog?"

If we choose to point blame and dwell in victimization, what we get
is anger and hurt as we are left without resolution. **We become powerful,
effective and fulfilled in our lives when we see ourselves as the cause of
what our lives look like in any particular moment.**

A mother at first spoke of how her "mean" husband was always putting her down and didn't allow her to give her opinion on most issues.
After several classes she realized that she promoted this situation by not

being assertive and by letting him get away with this behavior. As the classes progressed, she began looking at the part she played in the situation. Eventually she started telling him how his comments made her feel and that she wasn't going to put up with it. For many years she "allowed" him to talk to her in a hurtful manner. She took responsibility for changing the pattern by speaking up.

In another instance, a woman was speaking sadly about the fact that in her culture it was basically acceptable for married men to have other lovers. I inquired, "Is this type of behavior okay with you?" She responded that she was getting tired of her husband seeing other women. I asked her how she created, promoted or allowed this type of behavior. She acknowledged promoting it by not speaking up and saying how it hurt her. The next session, she reported that she told her husband how hurt she was. He denied any wrongdoing but they both knew the truth. She demanded that he be faithful. Over the next month, she reported that he treated her with a lot more respect — basically, the respect that she now demanded.

One of my high school students, Lauren, summed up this lesson on her final exam when she wrote, "I realize how much responsibility I have in certain situations, and rather than blame others, I look inside myself to see how I have brought it upon myself. **If I do this, I am in control of my life. If I blame others, they are controlling me.**"

YOU ARE THE ENVIRONMENT CHILDREN GROW UP IN

What we are communicating to our students in each moment is how we feel, which originates from what we are thinking. Masterful Teaching is about becoming aware of and taking responsibility for this internal environment. In every moment, these emotions are creating the classroom environment. Young children are very sensitive — they are like sponges absorbing and then reacting to everything in their environment. Researchers have observed what has been termed the "switching phenomenon." When we are under stress, the electrical polarity of our body is "switched." When an infant is in contact with parents who are constantly stressed, or when a mother is under stress while her child is in utero, the child's electrical polarity is also constantly being switched. Children, especially infants, are very susceptible to being weakened because they don't have the capacity to filter out what is negative from what is positive. This electrical imbalance or reversed polarity has been repeatedly noted in people with chronic fatigue, depression, cancer, autoimmune diseases and ADHD.

When we think negative thoughts and feel anger, our students are learning in an angry environment. When we view our students critically through the eyes of judgment, they are being taught in an unsafe environment.

The emotional quality of our classroom environment is affected by our attitude toward our students the same way their home environment is affected by the attitudes of their family members. Children who speak disrespectfully to their teachers are usually being raised in a home where parents speak disrespectfully to their children and/or to each other and where the parents don't demonstrate the resolve to speak up and not tolerate their child's disrespectful tone of voice. Children will grow strong in a nurturing environment — one that provides caring, understanding and loving attention. It's like a rose bush that responds to watering, care and an understanding of its growth cycle.

Studies related to how television affects our students' intellectual environment have shown that the brain can function on two very distinct levels: a "responding level" and a "thinking level." The rapid stimulation of TV locks the brain into "responding" mode, which eliminates the possibility of reflection, analytical thought, intellectual challenge and sustained or focused attention. As time in front of the television increases (the average American viewer spends 28 hours a week watching TV), viewers experience shorter attention spans, an impaired capacity to stick with a problem, reduced comprehension of complexities in language and diminished listening ability. Video games have a similar effect. The responsibility lies with the parents to determine how many hours a day their children watch television and play video games.

Parents are not the only influence in their children's lives, but children raised in a home environment of love, caring and empathy have very different beliefs about who they are compared to children raised in an environment permeated with anger, tension, judgment and fear.

LIFE IS EASY WHEN IT'S EASY, BUT...

You've had a brutal day at work, it's 95 degrees, the humidity is 95 percent, and you've spent the last 45 minutes on a crowded bus without air conditioning. You're already in a bad mood as you walk into your house and observe your 16-year-old daughter on the phone oblivious to the music blasting in the living room. Think about the thoughts and emotions you would have, given your existing mood. Not pretty, I bet. Now imagine walking into the same situation after just being told you received an unexpected pay raise at work and your best friend gave you a ride home in her beautiful new air conditioned car. Your thoughts, emotional state and reaction to your daughter and her music would most likely be quite different.

We are responsible for our moods and the consequences of the actions we take depending on our moods. Moods don't come from the outside. Rather, they develop from choices in thinking that we make regarding the events in our lives.

For example, earlier today I went out to mail a package. After driving the two-mile dirt road that leads from my house to the main road, I realized that I had forgotten a book that I wanted to include in the package. I raced home (the post office was closing soon) only to discover that I had never brought the book to my house in the first place. I then raced back to the post office and mailed the package. Returning to my car I heard a hissing sound being made by air escaping where a sharp rock had punctured my tire. The air was leaking slowly. I got into my car and started driving to the repair shop. On the way there I got behind a school bus. A trip that should have taken three minutes instead took ten. The mechanic was able to patch the tire but said I would need a new one because all the air had leaked out and the sidewall had collapsed and been damaged.

I drove to the tire store to find out that they no longer had my size tire. The story doesn't end here, but I'll stop.

Now, was it the tire's fault that I was in a bad mood? Did the school bus cause my emotional state? Or was it thoughts like, "I have no luck," "God is punishing me" and "life sucks" that caused me to be emotionally upset? I think you'll agree that I chose the negative thoughts which, in turn, produced my bad mood. In fact, for about 30 seconds I indulged in these negative thoughts and emotions but I soon snapped out of it and began to laugh.

The challenge always occurs when things get tough. The most important thing to do when we're in a bad mood is to observe and notice that we are in a bad mood. Knowing this gives us the choice to react from this place or to take a "time out" and relax before we proceed. A short time out isn't always enough to change our mood. Sometimes we need to read a book, exercise, listen to calming music, take a warm bath, or walk around the block to reestablish some semblance of peace inside of ourselves. How we relate to any issue determines whether we're going to create a bad mood or a good mood. As always, the choice is ours.

75

RESPONSIBILITY

1. WRITE DOWN AT LEAST ONE SITUATION WHERE YOU FELT PICKED ON, TREATED UNFAIRLY OR BLAMED FOR SOMETHING THAT YOU FELT WASN'T YOUR FAULT. WRITE THE SITUATION DOWN AS IF YOU WERE A VICTIM.

2. WRITE ABOUT THE SAME SITUATION FROM THE VIEWPOINT WHERE YOU CREATED, PROMOTED OR ALLOWED THE SITUATION TO HAPPEN. ALSO, LOOK AT THE CHOICES YOU MADE IN YOUR REACTION TO THE SITUATION. WRITE DOWN POSSIBLE CHOICES THAT YOU COULD HAVE MADE THAT MAY HAVE BEEN MORE BENEFICIAL TO YOURSELF AND OTHERS.

EDUCATION FOR TRANSFORMATION

PARTICIPANTS' COMMENTS

- A mother was really upset. Her son came home with terrible grades in three out of five junior high school classes. He said it wasn't his fault; the teachers just didn't like him. He had an excuse for every poor grade. The mother explained that in the past, when her son had problems with teachers in school, she would go and find out why the teachers were picking on him. It became obvious to her and everyone else in the class how she promoted her son's victim consciousness by supporting him when he blamed his teachers for his poor grades.

- A middle school dean reported his experience of teaching a course after a five-year absence from the classroom. "That first class was horrible. After ten minutes there was no discipline — the kids were all over the place. That night I was really angry. I blamed the school, the parents and the 'youth of today' for the unruly behavior."

  "After our class on responsibility, I looked at myself as the cause of the students' disrespect. When I did this, I realized that not having prepared a lesson plan for the first class may have contributed to the chaos in the room. The next time I met with my students I spent a considerable amount of time preparing for the class. The tone and the behavior of the students were totally transformed."

- A woman said that her husband was told to stop smoking by his doctor because he had pre-malignant cells present after a biopsy. He continued to smoke which upset her a great deal. I asked her how old he was. She said that he was 52. Although it was difficult to do, she needed to see her husband as responsible for his own actions.

- Several years ago I was thinking about starting a school based on the principles that I now present in my class. I spent a considerable amount of time traveling to schools around the country to observe teachers who were exemplary in what they taught. When I went to a

Middle School in South Central Los Angeles I was told by the administrators and other teachers to observe a certain math teacher. When I sat in his class I was impressed by the total absorption of the students. After class I asked him why he was such a successful teacher.

He responded, "The average student who enters the seventh grade at this school has achieved a third grade math level. I know that each and every student is capable of achieving a ninth grade math level by the time they complete the ninth grade. More often than not these students achieve that level of expectation. I have taken time to develop interesting and motivating lesson plans that incorporate hands on experimentation. I have also taken the responsibility of extending myself to my students by providing my home telephone number in order to address any problems or difficulties they may be facing."

7

FORGIVENESS

Forgiveness is one of the greatest gifts we can give to ourselves.

A father's lengthy and angry response when asked, "Who do you need to forgive?" can provide us with a good starting point for the exploration of this very important principle.

"I will never forgive my brother-in-law," he said. "We had a fight just before he married my sister. He felt that I thought that he was not good enough for her. Words led to threats, threats became blows and it ended up in an all out fight. Although I see him at family functions at least twice a year, I haven't spoken to him since the incident occurred more than twelve years ago."

After further discussion, this father revealed that he felt sad whenever he saw his brother-in-law and that it had definitely had a negativel effect on his relationship with his sister, with whom he had previously been very close. He now realized that he was demonstrating a "revenge" or "eye for an eye" response. I pointed out that there are perceived advantages to every choice we make. Some potential benefits to responding in a vengeful way might include:

- Blaming others
- Not taking responsibility for our part in what happened in the situation
- Defending innocence .... Proclaiming that everyone else is guilty
- Being right...It is the others who are wrong
- Believing that the world is unfair and people are hurt without reason
- Justifying our bitterness, anger and rage
- Not having to examine the part we played in the situation
- Feeling betrayed

The problem with these so-called "benefits" is they result in decreased love and vitality. In the same situation forgiveness is an alternate response that we can choose which offers these potential outcomes:

- Taking responsibility for our part in the situation
- Choosing to let go of feeling betrayed
- Beginning to heal our hurt and experiencing increased vitality
- Being aware that harmony is more important than being right and declaring the other person wrong
- Learning through compassion the lessons that the situation has to teach us rather than justifying our anger and rage

When we stop blaming others and take responsibility, we experience the increased vitality and love that healing brings. In contrast, revenge keeps us living in the past, attached to our hatred and unable to heal. **We hurt ourselves deeply in order to justify hurting someone else and being right.**

By not forgiving we can expect:	By forgiving we can expect:
1. Getting to be right by blaming others	1. Inner peace, love, empathy and vitality
2. Experiencing bitterness and rage	2. Learning from our experiences
3. Feeling Betrayal and Inner Pain	3. Healing and the acceptance of what is

BUT I THOUGHT THAT...

There are several common misconceptions regarding the act of forgiveness. Many people believe that the other person must apologize first before forgiveness can even be considered. This is a false premise. Not only does the other person not have to apologize first- he doesn't even have to be alive in order for forgiveness to occur. Forgiveness doesn't depend at all on the other person. **Forgiveness is an internal process that makes the necessary room in the heart for empathy.**

Many people view forgiveness as something nice we do for someone else (who doesn't deserve it in the first place). In reality when we forgive we release the negativity we are feeling for the other person. We let go of them. Without forgiveness we continue to carry the people we have not forgiven around with us. Scientists have observed an elevated heart rate and higher blood pressure in people who are trapped in their negativity. On the other hand, when we forgive, we experience internal calm and a healing of the part of ourselves that has been hurt. **More than an act of kindness to another, forgiveness is an act of kindness towards ourselves.**

Another misconception is the belief that when we forgive someone we are condoning his or her behavior. There is always the choice to forgive and at the same time make it clear that we do not appreciate the behavior. In fact , we can forgive and choose not to interact with that person anymore.

Often we are disappointed when feelings of anger and hatred reappear upon seeing, hearing or thinking about a person or situation. **Forgiveness is usually not a one-time event, but an ongoing process that often requires the experiencing and acceptance of a great deal of anger.**

81

I WAS BETRAYED

Betrayal seems to be a key issue in many situations that provoke anger, retaliation and non-forgiveness. **We take other peoples' behavior personally and call it betrayal when, in fact, they are really just doing what they have always done.** If we observe closely, we will most likely see that the person who is habitually breaking his agreements with us, has done the same to others. When we realize this fact, we have the choice to judge them for their behavior or to simply accept them for who they are. Again, it's always our choice.

SELF-FORGIVENESS

For many of us, forgiving ourselves can be even more challenging than forgiving others. Ask yourself, "What haven't I forgiven myself for?" For example, a very caring parent said she had a hard time forgiving herself for yelling at her child. She was hard on herself and judged herself as abusive and inconsiderate. On one level she could forgive herself for her actions. On a deeper level she needed to forgive herself for judging herself so harshly. Think about it. Being inconsiderate or abusive in not who we are. They are two behaviors among many that we are capable of manifesting. We need to realize that at any particular moment, we are all capable of any type of behavior. Destructive behavior and mistakes can be viewed as an opportunity to learn and grow or as an opportunity to beat ourselves up... As always, the choice is ours.

FORGIVENESS EXERCISE

YOU'RE ALWAYS HURT BY THE ONE YOU LOVE

1. AT THE TOP OF A PIECE OF PAPER, WRITE THE NAME OF SOME-
   ONE WITH WHOM YOU USED TO BE CLOSE BUT WITH WHOM,
   BECAUSE OF TENSION, YOU NO LONGER COMMUNICATE. THIS
   PERSON COULD BE A RELATIVE, EX-LOVER, EX-SPOUSE, EX-
   FRIEND, ETC. YOU KNOW-ONE OF THOSE "EX'S".

2. UNDER THIS PERSON'S NAME, MAKE TWO SEPARATE LISTS –
   ONE FOR GOOD QUALITIES, THE OTHER FOR BAD. CONSIDER
   STRENGTHS AND WEAKNESSES REGARDING QUALITIES SUCH
   AS: SENSE OF HUMOR, INTELLIGENCE, INTEGRITY, KINDNESS,
   EMPATHY, HONESTY, PHYSICAL ATTRACTIVENESS, ETC.

GOOD QUALITIES   BAD QUALITIES   83

WHAT DID YOU DISCOVER?

More often than not, that once-close person with whom we now can't communicate, is someone who we feel has hurt us and whom we have not forgiven. **It is impossible to communicate openly with someone we have not forgiven.**

This exercise also helps us acknowledge the positive qualities that we have appreciated in another and accept the qualities that we may have judged to be negative. In most cases, the person who we hate so much is someone we once loved. **The anger that is often felt is not the opposite of love, but actually a part of love.** Beneath anger is hurt and lying beneath the hurt is love. Acknowledging both the love and hurt creates the possibility of forgiveness and the subsequent sense of well being that comes from letting go. I am not saying that everyone can change their attitude from hatred to forgiveness overnight. It can be a long process, often requiring counseling and the processing of a great deal of emotion. What I hope, though, is that this chapter will bring the awareness that forgiveness is always an option and a choice. Lastly, I hope that you are now motivated to forgive, understanding that if you choose to no one will benefit more than you.

HOME ASSIGNMENT #7

FORGIVENESS OF SELF AND OTHERS

1. WHAT HAVE YOU NOT FORGIVEN YOURSELF FOR?

2. WHAT HAS SOMEONE ELSE NOT FORGIVEN YOU FOR?

3. WHO HAVEN'T YOU FORGIVEN?

4. WHY DO WE NEED TO FORGIVE?

WHAT WE GET BY:

NOT FORGIVING

* Get to be right
* No responsibility
* Blame
* Justify bitterness & rage
* Justify betrayal
* Inner pain, no healing

FORGIVING

* Inner peace
* Lessons learned
* Take responsibility
* Love and Vitality
* No betrayal, just what is
* Healing

PARTICIPANTS' COMMENTS

- When asked, "What have you not forgiven yourself for?" a mother from Nigeria responded that she had received two messages from her uncle in her homeland. She loved this man deeply but decided to wait until the weekend to call him back because it was much cheaper. When she called back, she was told that he had just passed away. She cried as she told this story and said that even though it had happened three years earlier, she still couldn't forgive herself for not calling back as soon as she had received the messages. She did admit, however, that in the past she had waited for the cheaper weekend rates to return calls, and that the message had given no indication that her uncle was sick.

  I pointed to another women in the group and asked the Nigerian woman, "If this woman did exactly what you did, could you forgive her?" She thought about it and realized that she could forgive the other woman. I asked: "Can you see the possibility of forgiving yourself?" She reflected and said, "It will be hard but I can see the possibility."

- A teacher from a foreign country said that although her reaction seemed extreme to many of her colleagues, she could not forgive her husband for smoking. "When I met my husband, he smoked. I hate the smell of smoke. I told him that if he smoked, I would not marry him. He said that he would quit and he did. But last year, I found out that he was smoking behind my back. At first he lied. Then he said that he would never do it again. Several months later, I found out that he was still smoking. I am thinking about getting a divorce because of this."

  A classmate responded, "My sister had the same problem with her husband. What she did was allow her husband to smoke outside the house but never inside the house. It seems to work for them."

  I asked, "Are you upset because he smokes or because he didn't keep his word?" She replied, "I want to divorce him because he betrayed me." I made her aware that the issue was his lying about smoking and not the act of smoking itself. The class also pointed out that she had essentially given him no choice but to lie. She never would have accepted the truth. We also discussed that her rationale for wanting a divorce may have been to get even by punishing her spouse. This is an example of the "eye for an eye" consciousness that we discussed earlier.

After pointing this out, I asked her, "I know the divorce will most likely hurt your husband deeply but what will you lose by not seeing him anymore?" She became quite sad and shared that she really loved him and that by leaving him she would be losing a great deal. Often, in our anger, we forget that when we take our heart away from another as a way of punishing them, we punish ourselves as well.

- Another teacher shared, "I need to deal with the guilt I have. Because of teaching, I am not able to spend a lot of time with my own young children. This is a very hard thing for me and I try to compensate by doing special things or buying them treats whenever I can. But then I feel guilty for spoiling them."

  Another teacher responded that being a teacher was a choice and one of the consequences of that choice was not being able to be a traditional housewife. But another consequence of being a teacher was that the lessons learned working with the children in school could make her a better parent to her own children.

- In response to "who do you need to forgive," a teacher said that she needed to forgive parents who make appointments and then do not show up. "I find it very upsetting when I rearrange my schedule to come into school early or stay late to accommodate a specific parent's schedule only to have them show up late or not show up at all. For the sake of my mental health and well-being, I need to not take their behavior personally. I need to accept that some people don't keep agreements, forgive them and realize that they will probably do the same thing if I make another appointment with them."

- A lesson on using mistakes as opportunities for growth was presented when a teacher spoke of her experience of returning to teaching after a five-year absence. "When the pangs and longings of my old profession arose in me, I thought it safe and best to enter at the lowest possible age group. I took a kindergarten position. I hated every minute of it because I felt like a baby-sitter. Two months were the most I could handle. I next taught a second grade class which I also didn't like. I was finally moved to grade six where I have spent four happy years.
This experience taught me about my comfort level. I am clearer about what age group is for me."

- A teacher was very upset after hearing from other teachers and students that the students in his class had given the substitute teacher a hard time when he was absent. He decided to punish the whole class. A couple of days later, he found out from the substitute that three students out of a class of thirty-two had misbehaved.

  He wrote, "At that point I felt I had made a poor decision in deciding to discipline the entire class. What I should have done was to not do anything until I spoke to the substitute and then deal with those students who had caused a disturbance on a one to one basis."

- I would like to share a personal experience. It is easy for me to forgive myself and apologize for behavior that I know was inappropriate. Some time ago, I had an argument with my girlfriend while we were visiting a beautiful foreign city. I just stormed off and we each toured the city alone. I got back to where we were staying six hours after she did because I had missed the train. We didn't speak until the next morning. When I woke up, I apologized and began to cry very deeply. This experience of apologizing was different from any other I had ever had. As I was crying, I was realizing and apologizing for any pain I had caused her or anyone else.

Since that experience I have become much kinder to her; not because I feel guilty, but because something deep inside of me was released by going to that level. Maybe the apologizing that was so easy for me is only one level of forgiveness. The profound healing I experienced arose from my feeling a deep level of remorse for any suffering I had ever inflicted on anyone, ever. I know it doesn't serve us to beat ourselves up but it does seem that experiencing and expressing our deep remorse has incredible value. What is your experience?

- This mother's sharing after doing the forgiveness homework was a profound demonstration of the power of forgiveness.

  "I realized for the first time that I looked at my 10-year-old son differently than my daughter. I didn't like what I saw because I saw his father's face who I never forgave for cheating on me. I broke down and cried. I felt so sad for my son and didn't like myself for being so cruel. When I recovered I saw that I needed to do what ever it took to forgive his father so I could be more loving to my son."

8

COMMUNICATION
IT AIN'T WHAT YOU SAY...OR IS IT?

We teach who we are. Children learn how to deal with others by observing how the adults in their lives communicate.

Experts who study communication tell us that there are three primary modes or styles of communication: passive, aggressive and assertive. Take a few minutes to answer the following questions to see how each mode is different, and to determine which style you use most often.

WHAT IS YOUR MODE OF COMMUNICATION?

CIRCLE THE RESPONSE THAT IS TRUEST FOR YOU.
Please answer openly and honestly by indicating how you actually are and not how you would like to be or how you would like to be seen.

Always true (at least 90% of the time)
Often true (75% of the time)
Sometimes true (50% of the time)
Rarely true (25% of the time)
Never true (less than 10% of the time)

1. *I enjoy meeting new people*
    Always   Often   Sometimes   Rarely   Never

2. *I have a right to say "no" to things I don't want to do*
    Always   Often   Sometimes   Rarely   Never

3. *I have a right to express my feelings*
   Always   Often   Sometimes   Rarely   Never

4. *A person can change how he or she gets along with others*
   Always   Often   Sometimes   Rarely   Never

5. *I have a right to ask for what I need*
   Always   Often   Sometimes   Rarely   Never

6. *It is easy for me to say "no" to things I don't want to do*
   Always   Often   Sometimes   Rarely   Never

7. *I don't let others boss me around*
   Always   Often   Sometimes   Rarely   Never

8. *It is easy for me to express negative feelings like anger*
   Always   Often   Sometimes   Rarely   Never

9. *I have trouble controlling my temper*
   Always   Often   Sometimes   Rarely   Never

10. *I am honest about my feelings with friends*
    Always   Often   Sometimes   Rarely   Never

INTERPRETING THE RESULTS

Let's score your answers to reveal your predominant mode of communication. On the next page we will define each mode.

SCORING TABLE

Always	5 points
Often	4 points
Sometimes	3 points
Rarely	2 points
Never	1 point

PASSIVITY SCALE
Using the scoring from above, add up your points from questions 1-9. A score of 27 or below indicates a **PASSIVE** communicator.

ASSERTIVENESS SCALE
Using the scoring table above, add up your points from questions 1-7. A score of 28 or above indicates an **ASSERTIVE** communicator.

AGGRESSIVENESS SCALE
Using the scoring table from above, add up your points from questions 7-9. A score of 12 or above indicates an **AGGRESSIVE** communicator.

The purpose of this scoring is not only to learn about your habitual mode of communication, but also to show that people are very different and can vary widely regarding their particular style of communication. If someone is passive, we need to be patient and encourage them to speak their truth. If they are the aggressive type, we need to help them get past the emotions they're feeling in order to communicate more effectively.

THE THREE PRIMARY MODES OF COMMUNICATING

(PASSIVE, AGGRESSIVE, ASSERTIVE)

In observing your mode of communication, you need to take into account that our style of communication often changes depending on who we are speaking to. You may be habitually passive with one person and consistently aggressive with someone else. For instance, you might be habitually aggressive with your mother but fall into a passive habit with your father. The key term here is "habitual pattern". A lot of times the "safe" people get our anger while the ones we fear get our silence. It's fine to choose to be passive sometimes and to choose to be aggressive at other times with a particular person. However, problems arise when we don't choose but, instead, communicate in a habitual pattern that usually does not serve us.

With this is mind, let's take a look at some of the thought patterns that are behind the different styles. Listed below are several "reasons" for being a passive communicator followed by a list of "reasons" for communicating aggresively. Circle any that apply to your interaction with anyone in your life.

Passive communication means not saying what you think, feel, need or want. When you are passive, you are putting another person's needs before your own because...

1. You are afraid to risk the consequences
2. You don't want to "make waves"
3. You think it's more important to be liked than to say what you want to say
4. You don't want to be noticed or call attention to yourself
5. You are afraid of being wrong
6. You don't believe in your right to express your wants, needs, feelings and opinions
7. You think another person's rights are more important than yours
8. You think it takes too much energy to say something that probably won't do any good anyway
9. You are influenced by your culture
10. You have allowed it to become a habit
11. You have been hurt by aggression and do not wish to hurt others
12. You feel that you will be hurt or taken advantage of if you express your feelings

Aggressive communication means saying what you think, feel, want or need without respecting the feelings of others. When you are aggressive, you are putting your own needs before the needs of others because...

1. You don't want to acknowledge the hurt behind your anger
2. You were never taught a different way to communicate
3. You don't want people having power or taking advantage of you
4. You find it easier to be aggressive
5. You have allowed it to become a habit
6. You want to control the situation
7. You don't like hearing "no"
8. You can't hold the feeling of anger inside of yourself so you release it on others

ASSERTIVE COMMUNICATION.....FINDING THE MIDDLE GROUND

Ideally, passive and aggressive styles can be replaced with assertive communication. This applies to every relationship in your life, whether it is with a family member, a friend or a co-worker. Assertive communicating means saying what you think, feel or want in a way that respects your needs as well as the needs of the other person because...

Assertive communication means saying what you think, feel or want in a way that respects your needs as well as the needs of the other person because...

1. You want to communicate in a way that respects others
2. You want to communicate in a straightforward, clear and non-threatening way
3. You want to communicate in a way that respects our own rights

The key to replacing an aggressive style with assertive communication is to communicate the hurt feeling rather than the anger. The key to replacing a passive style with assertive communication is to communicate the hurt feeling rather than not saying anything at all. **It requires**

courage to be vulnerable and speak our truth. The "ABC" formula provides a practical tool for promoting more peaceful relationships through assertive communication:

> A – When you say or do...
> B – I "feel"...
> C – I "need"...

This formula, besides promoting your own assertive communication, can be particularly helpful when conflicts arise.

Passive types attempt to resolve conflict by not saying anything. Often these people are not in touch with their needs and feelings in the moment. This lack of awareness usually is the results of internal moral judgments as to which feelings are acceptable and which needs are justifiable. Is it selfish to need respect, love, security, or to be heard? Or maybe, is it our right as human beings to express and fulfill our needs? These are questions that people who are habitually not speaking their truth might want to ask themselves. **Again, the key to having successful relationships is the ability to experience what you are feeling and communicate that feeling to other people in a respectful manner; i.e., assertive communication.** This applies to every relationship in your life, whether it is with your spouse, your children, your friends, your co-worker or anyone we interact with.

When you look more closely at aggressive patterns of communication, you will see that anger is most often a response to a specific hurt, such as feeling disrespected, being taken advantage of, not being heard or feeling betrayed. The anger is always one step removed from the hurt. The way to move from a response of anger to assertive communication is to acknowledge and express the hurt you are feeling, first to yourself and then to the other person. You will experience very different outcomes if you say, "I feel betrayed, disrespected, taken advantage of or hurt" rather than blowing up and yelling. **Assertive communication produces an inner sense of integrity because you are speaking your truth and at the same time promotes real intimacy because you're being vulnerable.**

EDUCATION FOR TRANSFORMATION

I'M NOT SUPPOSED TO GET SO ANGRY AT SOMEONE I LOVE

It's my experience that the people we love the most (family members, friends, significant others) bring out our anger the most. You might think that if you love someone, you're not supposed to get angry at them. But this belief does not withstand the test of reality. Loved ones have the ability to hurt us at the deepest level exactly because we love them so much. **Anger is not the opposite of love. It is a response to the hurt we feel because we love.** Because we are easily hurt by these "special" people, we are often the most vulnerable around them.

It takes a lot of courage to be vulnerable and express our hurt. Kids today spend a lot of energy acting tough, wearing "gangsta" clothes, dressing in black, getting tattoos and having different body parts pierced. But this tough façade is really the opposite of being vulnerable. It's more like a form of fear — the fear of being real and expressing how they really feel. Similarly, the word "whatever" has become a mantra for many youngsters who would rather pretend to be cool and aloof than express what is going on inside of them.

When we communicate how we feel and what we need in a respectful manner, we're showing our students a better way — a way that promotes loving relationships and success in life.

FEELINGS FOLLOW THOUGHTS...BUT TO FEEL IS REAL

Hurt is what drives anger. My habitual response might be to get angry and to yell at my girlfriend when I see her talking to another guy. The assertive approach would be to tell her that when she flirts with another guy I feel jealous and abandoned.

It gets a little tricky when we realize that behind the hurt is often a negative thought. Some psychologists suggest an alternative approach: looking at the negative thinking that causes the jealousy in the first place. A belief such as, "If she talks to another guy it means that she is going to leave me," might be generating the hurt and anger. When we realize this, we might be able to better understand the situation, calm our emotions, and not even have to communicate our jealousy. This way of viewing situations makes us responsible for our behavior rather then blaming others for our emotional state.

I have friends who are able to go to this level of understanding in many situations that have the potential for emotional upheaval. In most cases, these individuals have been working on themselves for a long time and have developed a deep understanding of their own as well as others' emotional nature. But for one friend in particular, it is easy for him to control his emotions because he is not in touch with how he feels. This is an example of behavior on the outside being generated by very different reasons on the inside. This form of non-vulnerability is very common in a society such as ours which prizes emotional control over emotional expression. We must be cautious when observing ourselves and others to see what is motivating behavior. Is it a suppressed fear of emotions or an advanced emotional understanding?

A vast majority of the teachers who participate in the Education for Transformation program are neither emotional masters nor control freaks. Rather, they are stuck in an aggressive or passive pattern of expression that produces a great deal of stress for themselves and others they interact with. The challenge for many is first to recognize their habitual style of communication and then to observe their feelings and communicate them in an assertive manner. This is very difficult to do, but **when an unconscious negative pattern of behavior is broken and a different choice is made, we feel a joy inside that comes from knowing we have done the right thing.**

FEED THE NEED

Along with feelings, we all have needs that must be internally acknowledged and communicated. Needs such as food, shelter and to be loved are common to all of us. The need to contribute to our own well-being and the well being of others, although extremely profound, is often not acknowledged. From an early age, girls are taught that their needs aren't that important, and that what is important is caring for and nurturing others. Boys are taught that in order to be strong they should endure hardship without showing pain and that they shouldn't have to rely on others for support. I have observed how differently boys and girls relate to someone who has been hurt during a sports activity. Girls will run over to an injured girl and try to help her whereas the boys will usually ignore a boy who is laying on the ground, expecting him to be "tough enough" to make it off the playing field on his own.

Along with recognizing and communicating our needs, it is also essential to understand the specific needs of others. Instead of recognizing children's needs, we often manipulate them by using guilt, fear, reward, punishment, shame and obligation. Manipulation based communication might work in the moment to get them to do what we want but in the long run it does not create an environment of trust, nor does it foster open relationships. For instance, a mother could tell her 14 year-old daughter that if she doesn't clean the dishes she will not be able to go to her best friend's birthday party.

Alternately the mother could balance her need to have support around the house with that her daughter's desire to contribute out of a need to be treated as an integral part of the family. When this happens an environment is created of sharing and helping each other as part of a cohesive family. After years of functioning in such an environment of trust, mutual respect and cooperation, the mother's communication might be, "I need your help with the dishes. I know you need to go to your friend's party. How can we make this work for both of us?" Creating a loving, respectful environment fulfills a very deep need for all students. Isn't that what we all wanted and needed when we were going to school?

HABIT VS. CONSCIOUS CHOICE

We can't possibly be effective in our lives if we fail to express our inner truth in a way that respects others. For this to happen, we must first become aware of what mode of communication we use. We need to observe the roles we play out of habit and consciously make new, more beneficial choices. As we get better at this, we can decide the outcome we want beforehand and communicate in a way that will achieve the desired result.

This was exemplified by Lewis, a participant in one of my classes. Lewis had a job in a warehouse where he was responsible for distributing and keeping track of expensive diagnostic equipment. The workers would sign the equipment out for a five-day period but they almost never returned it on time. Lewis would have to hunt them down and nag them which made him very upset. So much so in fact, that when he saw the workers hanging out in the parking lot before work, he would get really angry.

After the class on communication, Lewis became more aware of his habitually angry response. He saw that all of his anger was getting him nowhere. He became more accepting and was able to joke with the other workers. When they explained why they usually returned the equipment late he was able to empathize. He told me, "Work became more enjoyable. You wouldn't believe it but the more calmly I asked them why the equipment was late instead of getting angry, the more often the equipment got back on time."

A mother from one of my classes shared how changing her usual mode of communication helped smooth things over with her daughter. "I observed that sometimes my pattern of communication with my daughter was too aggressive," she said. "When I saw that chores weren't done or homework was started late, I would lose my temper. I often began my communication with, 'Didn't I tell you to do this?' or 'Why isn't this done yet?' or 'Why are you still sitting here?' Things would go downhill from there. She would get angry or I would get angry and nothing would be gained. When I began to approach my daughter differently by explaining her responsibilities and telling her how I felt when she was not honoring her agreement, things began to change." **It is not easy to change habitual patterns and being gentle with yourself is very important, especially at times when you think you have "blown it".**

Another student shared that all he had to do to win an argument with his girlfriend was to tell her to "get out" and she would give in. His aggressiveness forced her to be passive. This is an example of manipulation, not open communication. If we care about a person, are we really serving them by playing games that give us power? Open and honest communication can strengthen a relationship because it lets each partner look at the issues that are contributing to their unconscious reactions. **One of the functions of a loving relationship is to help both persons free themselves from habitual patterns that do not serve them.**

AGGRESSIVE VS. PASSIVE

Often, we respond to someone in an aggressive way because it gives us a feeling of control over a situation that makes us uncomfortable. A lot of kids are aggressive because they don't want others to be in charge of them or to take advantage of them. But who really has control when you get angry, you or the other person? My experience is that when I get angry, the other person has control over me. He or she is controlling my mood. As far as anger giving you power, any martial arts instructor will tell you that it's easy to defeat a person when they are angry.

There are many ways that responding aggressively can backfire as a way of communicating. Some people think that screaming their feelings is a surefire way to be heard but, in fact, it's usually a way to make others tune you out. A third grade teacher in one of my workshops offered a good example. She shared a story about two elementary school students, Maci and Alyssa, who were always arguing at lunchtime. During one of these arguments the teacher approached Maci, who was very upset and started yelling as she told her version of what had happened.

"When this happens, I often react by telling Maci very harshly not to yell in my face. This time I chose to employ a different tactic by stopping her and explaining that I could not listen to her when she spoke like that. When she began again she was still very hostile and loud. I stopped her again and expressed to her how I felt when she yelled. I further explained to everyone else involved that if they wanted people to give a positive response to what they were saying, they would have to say it in a way that was not offensive to the person trying to listen. I told Maci that I would listen when she was ready to speak to me in a more respectful manner. She took a moment or two to collect herself and then explained what had happened in a calmer tone. I felt that her relaxed tone helped, in part, to defuse the situation."

On the other end of the spectrum are people who react passively. Passive types generally try to resolve conflict by not saying anything. They might back down during an argument or not speak up for themselves if they feel they're being mistreated. Some kids are passive in other ways. They might get straight A's on their homework and quizzes but they never raise their hand in class to answer a question. Often they don't share because they are afraid of being wrong or bringing attention to themselves. Many of these children have the intelligence and discipline to be leaders but this won't happen until they develop the courage to speak their truth.

Once we understand and can observe our habitual patterns of communication, we can choose which pattern serves us the best in any given situation. The assertive approach is preferable in most situations, but for those of us who are habitually aggressive, a little passivity can go a long way. Likewise, for a passive person, choosing to get angry every once in a while may be just fine. Whatever your habitual mode of communication, the goal is to step back, observe and then choose what works best in any given situation.

DO YOU WANT PEACE OR WAR?

To understand how powerful we are as creators, think of two prizefighters. If Lenox Lewis is scheduled to fight Mike Tyson on March 1 and Tyson says on February 28 that he is not going to fight, will there be a fight? No, there won't. We all share the same power to decide whether there will be peace or war in each moment of our lives.

One student summed up the lesson on communication by saying, "The most valuable thing I learned from the course is that I can be assertive without hurting others and without the fear of being disliked. Discovering that I have a choice to respond to hurt in a fashion that makes war or peace has totally changed how I relate to others."

COMMUNICATION

1. OBSERVE YOUR HABITUAL MODE OF COMMUNICATION WITH A STUDENT, SPOUSE, CO-WORKER OR ANY OTHER SIGNIFICANT PERSON. RECORD THE CHANGES YOU MAKE WHEN YOUR COMMUNICATION BECOMES ASSERTIVE RATHER THAN AGGRESSIVE OR PASSIVE.

- Changes made

104

- Result of changes

2. OBSERVE AND RECORD YOUR PATTERN OF GETTING ANGRY WHEN YOU DONT GET WHAT YOU WANT. THIS CAN OCCUR AT A RED LIGHT, WHEN A PERSON SAYS "NO" TO YOU OR IN MANY OTHER SITUATIONS.

DO YOU WANT WAR OR PEACE?

EDUCATION FOR TRANSFORMATION

PARTICIPANTS' COMMENTS

- Since taking the course, a woman shared that she had learned more beneficial ways to approach issues that come up with her daughter. However, she was still having difficulty communicating with her husband and was afraid that if she spoke her truth it would create conflict and she "did not want to make waves". I told her that the price we pay for not making waves is a loss of vitality and less then optimal health. Withholding our truth is a major cause of illness and feeling unhappy. She was encouraged to communicate her true feelings to her husband.

- A teacher shared in her homework: "I see a change in my approach towards Delfin (one of her students). I was habitually aggressive with him. After our class on choices in communication, I find myself using a more assertive approach. For example, a week ago, if Delfin asked to borrow a pencil I would have aggressively reprimanded him for not being prepared for class. But now I reflect for a second or two and use a kinder, more assertive approach before lending him the pencil. At this point I believe he may be a little confused with my behavior, but I feel less stress when using this assertive approach."

- A mother shared, "Friday I asked my mom to be ready to go the hairdresser. When I arrived she was not ready which was going to make me late for my appointment. I would normally yell and be very aggressive with her because of her inconsiderateness. What I did differently was that when my mom came into the car, I informed her that the next time she made me late for an appointment, she would have to find another means of transportation. I said this in an assertive non-threatening way."

105

- In speaking about an assistant teacher who was constantly disrespecting her, another teacher commented, "I have created this problem with my assistant teacher, because if I had been assertive in my interaction with her, she would have been aware that I do not like what has been going on. But since I decided to be passive, I promoted the situation and she took advantage of it. I have learned that it is better to address an issue rather than to pretend that it does not exist. I have now decided not to take any action of hers for granted but to tell her what I think about anything she does that affects me emotionally."

- A teacher told about the process he used to change the inappropriate behavior of a student named Earl. The teacher stated: "I have used all the conventional corrective methods for dealing with Earl with only temporary results. In my attempt to change my communication from aggressive to assertive. I decided that any behavior acted out by this student would not result in an argument between us. I would make him aware of my displeasure (quietly but firmly) and arrange to discuss it between classes or after school. I also confiscated objects that were a distraction to him and others, i.e. unrelated subject material, food items, a walkman, etc.

  "In private, I questioned him about his family seeking to find some connection to his constant need for attention and his home environment. He shared quite a bit about his personal life. "I attended a talent show where he performed and I complimented him on his performance. He seemed appreciative. We have come to an understanding regarding his classroom behavior."

- A teacher shared this experience: "There are three students in my homeroom that generally create a problem at dismissal by coming late to class after helping another teacher. This teacher gives them late passes for being held over for no more than three minutes. They abuse this privilege by coming to homeroom ten minutes late and detaining the whole class. I used to handle this situation in a passive manner by telling them that the entire class was being inconvenienced and they should help the other teacher in the morning instead of at the end of the day. My instructions had no effect on their lateness. Last Wednesday, the three students came to homeroom while the class was on line outside. They wanted to get their books and jackets from the classroom. I told them they had to find a custodian to let them in and that they were being put in detention for being late. With a bit of difficulty, they were able to find a custodian. They have been on time ever since. Because they are nice kids and good students, I was too passive with them. I had to become more assertive in order for their behavior to change."

This story brings up an important point: There is nothing innately bad about being passive or aggressive. The problem occurs when the pattern of being habitually passive or aggressive does not serve ourselves or others. For habitually passive people, sometimes it is necessary and positive to be aggressive. On the other hand, for those of us who find it easy to be aggressive, playing a passive role can be very insightful and therapeutic.

- In his communication homework assignment, a middle school dean gave an account of his interaction with a habitual troublemaker named Chris: "Normally when Chris is brought to me for cutting class, I don't even listen to him. I simply say, 'Now you're out of here. I'm calling your mother and throwing you out the door.' When Chris tries to explain his side of the story, I say 'Close your mouth. You're supposed to be in class and you're not. Case closed.'

"One day, instead of waiting for Chris to mess up, I called him into my office and told him that he is a bright kid who obviously cares about his education given the fact that he shows up every week for Saturday Academy. I pointed out that there were only twenty-five days of school left and that all he had to do to graduate was to come to school, go to class and stay out of trouble. I also told him that if I did not get good reports or if I caught him cutting class, I would have to send him home. The choice was left entirely up to him.

"After a week, Chris went to detention once for being late: but he survived the week without cutting class or being sent home."

- A teacher spoke about insulting a class that was doing poor work and not behaving in an exemplary manner. She constantly complained and spoke to the group as if they were stupid. "Students would get attitudes with me and they would challenge me. Their behavior made it hard for me to enjoy teaching. Finally, I realized that my negativity towards the class was the problem and I needed to display a different approach. I therefore decided to be pleasant and use less sarcasm. This approach has been working. The students seem to feel more comfortable with me and are starting to like me more and as a result they are doing better work."

- Responding to the second home assignment question, a teacher wrote about Hasan, a third grade student who did everything in his power to upset her: "I notice that Hasan smiles whenever I get angry. Getting angry in front of the kids really is upsetting. But his smiling drives me nuts." I commented that young boys often love their teachers and get attention by upsetting them. This is what I did when I was eight. I suggested that she tell Hasan that it really hurts and upsets her when he misbehaves. Guilt works....sometimes.

- A teacher reported, "Craig is a resistant learner, meaning he resists everything I try to teach him. Craig and I usually go head to head for the whole period. This interaction was really beginning to wear me down. What I started to do was relax, lower my voice, and take away any personal feelings I had about his attitude toward learning. I told him that if he didn't want to learn and participate, he could just sit there, but he wasn't allowed to disturb others. He would receive the grade he earned. As a result of my new approach, my stress level went down and our relationship became less volatile."

DO YOU WANT PEACE OR WAR?

9

THE QUALITY TEACHER

"The very intention to teach is an act of love."   Frank Siccone

The most important variable in a child's academic success is the student-teacher interaction. The teacher is a nurturer, a reinforcer, an assessor, a challenger, a listener, an observer, a caretaker, a motivator, a counselor, a role model, a learning mediator, an information-giver, a storyteller and a learner. In this chapter we will focus on those factors which have the greatest influence on the instructional-learning process. The emphasis will be on increasing the students' performance by raising the overall effectiveness of the teacher.

1.   **STUDENTS WILL RISE TO OUR LEVEL OF EXPECTATION** It is worthwhile to repeat an experience that I shared in the chapter on Taking Responsibility. When I first started out in education, I wanted to open a school with a foundation based on the principles of self-mastery. I went to schools all over the United States and observed educators who were doing exemplary work. When I entered a school I would ask the administrators and teachers, "Who is your most inspiring teacher?" While visiting a middle school in Los Angeles I observed a highly recommended math teacher who truly exemplified the influence that a teacher's attitude has on his or her students. I sat in his class of totally engrossed ninth graders and watched a master at work. After class I asked him why he was so successful. This was his response: "Most of my students enter the seventh grade at a third grade math level. By the time these kids graduate from the ninth grade I know that they will be functioning at a ninth grade math level. I hold this vision and do the work necessary so that they graduate at this level."

Another excellent example of the correlation between expectation and results occurred in a school in England. An incorrectly programmed computer labeled a class of "bright" kids "dumb" and supposedly "dumb" kids "bright." The teachers used this faulty information while teaching these students. Five months later the school decided to measure the students again without telling anyone what had happened. The "bright" kids went down in IQ points. They had been treated as mentally slow, uncooperative and poor learners. Over the same period the scores for the "dumb" kids went up. The teachers had treated them as if they were bright and they had high individual expectations.

When questioned the teachers said at first that their lessons were not working with the kids they thought were bright. Taking responsibility, they changed their lessons in order to produce better results.

When I teach I hold the vision that my students are capable of transforming their lives by understanding and then applying the principles I present. I have also observed myself holding irrational beliefs that work against the attainment of this vision. If a student looks a certain way then I have assumed that they probably won't do the work necessary to succeed in my class. Eighteen-year-old Gregory strutted into my class the first day with baggy pants worn around his knees, a big gold chain, and a rag tied around his head. My first thought was that I was in for a hard time. As the days went on Gregory turned out to be one of the most respectful, insightful and emotionally intelligent students I had ever taught. My experience with Gregory provided a real learning for me.

Most of us have judgments based on physical appearance, ethnicity and social-economic or cultural factors that can influence our expectations of a student's performance. Our job is to recognize and observe these prejudices when they occur and to let them go so we can give our students the opportunity that they rightfully deserve.

2. **WE TEACH WHO WE ARE AS WELL AS WHAT WE KNOW.** This has been the overall theme of this book. But it never hurts to say it one more time. When we exemplify assertive communication instead of being habitually passive or aggressive with our students, they experience and learn what it is to communicate assertively. Similarly, our students learn masterful listening, how to resolve conflict peacefully and compassion for others by observing how we operate in each of these areas.

We can talk about what it means to be a good listener, but there is nothing like the experience of being with a masterful listener. It's much like learning how to inline skate by skating behind someone who is great at it.

3. **WE ARE RESPONSIBLE FOR WHAT GOES ON IN OUR CLASS.** There is a tendency to blame the administration, large classes, parental apathy and children's overall lack of motivation for the poor academic performance of our students. These factors can all have an influence but we as teachers can transcend these variables by taking responsibility for how our students perform. When our students are inattentive or not cooperating, instead of blaming them, we need to ask ourselves in the moment, "How can I present this material in a way that my students will be more engaged and better able to understand what I am trying to convey?"

There are several other practical steps that we can take to create a better learning environment by taking responsibility for bringing more enthusiasm, excellence and fun into the classroom. We can:

- Develop interesting and motivating lesson plans that incorporate hands-on experience.
- Conference with parents when their child is not performing at an acceptable level.
- Be more creative with our lessons by applying new approaches if what we are doing is not producing the desired results.

- Give our students our home telephone number if we think it's appropriate.
- Give clear explanations, expectations and directions.
- Read books and take continuing education courses in order to better understand and adapt our teaching methods to the age specific learning abilities of our students.
- Introduce cooperative learning techniques into our classroom.
- Take advantage of training opportunities to make us more effective on a personal as well as professional level.
- Exemplify masterful listening, assertive communication, taking responsibility and forgiveness as a way of creating an uplifting class room environment.

4. **A DEEP LEVEL OF CARING FOR OUR STUDENTS IS A NECESSARY FOUNDATION FOR BEING A SUCCESSFUL TEACHER.** We are in a service profession. We need to continually remind ourselves that serving those we teach is our main function as a teacher. One important way to do this is to keep in mind our students' basic needs. Every one of our students has a basic need:

- For fun
- For acceptance
- For expression
- To influence their education through feedback
- To be acknowledged and feel competent
- For belonging
- For power
- For freedom
- For security
- To be presented with material that has relevance in their lives

Students work hard for teachers they care for, have fun with, who give them respect and who let them think and act independently. When students are given the freedom and power to evaluate the class by way of giving constructive feedback, not only do they feel more empowered, but our teaching performance will vastly improve as well.

5. **APPRECIATING AND RESPECTING OUR STUDENTS IS A WAY OF SUPPORTING AND NURTURING THEM.** Students do not come to school in a vacuum. Many are dealing with family issues that negatively influence their academic performance. An elementary school teacher's experience illustrates this point: "There is a boy in my class who is emotionally disturbed. He would bite himself and not care about the damage he was doing to himself. He continually interrupted class and could not remain on task for more than five minutes. I was not very nice to him and I prayed everyday that he would not come to school. A month ago, I decided to speak with his family, his therapist and his social worker to find out what was wrong with him. I found out that his mother is a drug addict and his father is in jail. Ever since I found this out I am able to show him more love and care. Because I am able to empathize with him, we have developed a nice relationship."

Many of us spend a great deal of class time dealing with our students' negative behavior. An important way to raise their self-esteem as well as acknowledge the fruits of our labors is to praise students when they work hard or do a good job.

6. **WE BETTER SERVE OUR STUDENTS BY SPENDING LESS TIME RANKING THEM AND MORE TIME HELPING THEM IDENTIFY AND CULTIVATE THEIR NATURAL GIFTS.** Most of us are accustomed to defining intelligence as it relates to English and Math, along the same lines as the College Board Examination. Dr. Howard Gardner in his theory of multiple intelligences, equates intelligence with problem solving skills, i.e. the ability to approach a situation in which a goal is to be obtained and

to locate an appropriate route to that goal. This goal (cultural product) can range from a scientific theory, to a musical composition, to a successful political campaign, to finding a way to bring peace to a part of one's life that is in turmoil. Dr. Gardner found through extensive neurological testing, brain research, psychological testing, subjective evaluations, and cross cultural studies, that there were actually seven types of intelligence that are independent of each other — each having its own strengths and constraints.

A) **Linguistic Intelligence**
People who excel in this type of intelligence experience clarity with language, an understanding of the meaning of words and sensitivity to the different functions of language such as it's potential to excite, convince or convey information. Writers, lawyers, politicians, public speakers and poets exemplify this type of intelligence.

B) **Logical Mathematical Intelligence**
These individuals demonstrate what is commonly referred to as scientific thinking. This is the ability to compare, contrast and synthesize information. People with this intelligence understand the world through a grasp of the actions one can perform on objects; the relations between those actions and the potential of these actions.

C) **Musical Intelligence**
This intelligence deals with the recognition of tonal patterns and a sensitivity to rhythms and beats. People with highly developed musical intelligence often hear tones and rhythms in their heads.

D) **Spatial (Visual) Intelligence**
Central to this intelligence is the ability to perceive the visual world accurately, to perform transformations and changes upon the initial perceptions and to be able to recreate aspects of this visual experience. Sculptors, visual artists, choreographers, set designers and chess players exhibit this type of intelligence.

E) **Bodily-Kinesthetic Intelligence**

This intelligence deals with physical movement and the knowledge of the body and how it operates. Swimmers, dancers, actors, and athletes demonstrate this type of intelligence.

F) **Interpersonal Intelligence**

This relates to the ability to notice and make distinctions regarding other individuals' moods, temperaments, motivations and intentions. The focus is on others, the mastery of the social role and relationships (organizations, groups, personal relations). People who excel as parents, teachers, counselors, organizational leaders and spouses exemplify this type of intelligence.

G) **Intrapersonal Intelligence**

This intelligence is defined by a well-developed sense of self. The core strength is the ability to access one's own feeling, the capacity to instantly discriminate among these feelings, to label them, and to draw upon them as a means of understanding and guiding one's behavior.

Multiple Intelligence Theory professes that there is no hierarchy to intelligence. In other words Michael Jordan (a fine example of a person possessing a very high level of Bodily Kinesthetic intelligence) is just as intelligent as Albert Einstein who demonstrated a high level of Logical Mathematical Intelligence. Likewise, Mikhail Baryshnikov (Bodily Kinesthetic) is every bit as intelligent as Longfellow (Linguistic Intelligence). This has practical application in the classroom in that students are viewed as being gifted (more intelligent) in particular areas. Dr. Gardner has said that "the single most important contribution education can make to a child's development is to help him toward a field where his talents best suit him, where he will be satisfied and competent...We should spend less time ranking children and more time helping them to identify their natural competencies and gifts."

7. **IT IS BETTER TO DIFFUSE RATHER THAN TO ADD TO THE TUR-MOIL OF A CHARGED SITUATION.** When a student is disrespectful or misbehaves in any way, we have the choice of ignoring the behavior, confronting the student in front of the class or speaking with the student after class. Confronting them in front of class usually leads to a power struggle. They want to look good and we want to show the class we have control. This dynamic is avoided if we discuss the problem privately after class. Furthermore, students feel connected — they have a group consciousness. When we choose to confront a student and battle with them in front of the class, there is a good chance that the other students will join together and support the student.

8. **STUDENTS NEED TO EXPERIENCE THE INTERNAL SATISFAC-TION THAT COMES FROM DOING QUALITY WORK RATHER THAN BEING EXCLUSIVELY MOTIVATED BY PUNISHMENT AND REWARDS.** In my experience, the majority of students do just enough work to get by. Students are just mirroring a society where mediocrity instead of excellence has become the norm. As a society we eat at fast food restaurants, watch boring programs on television, listen to uncreative repetitious music, work at jobs that don't bring a deep level of satisfaction, worship the body instead of the mind or spirit, and are more concerned with gossip than true creativity.

As teachers we have the opportunity to show our students a different way, by creating a classroom environment that demonstrates and demands quality. Again, we teach who we are. One important way we can promote quality is to demonstrate quality by developing lesson plans that are clear, creative and thought provoking. Another way is by having our room be a place of inspiration and beauty. This can be done by displaying art, the excellent work of students and thought-provoking quotations. Other ways of bringing quality into the classroom include:

- Being clear and giving examples of what we expect from any assignment
- Having students evaluate each others work
- Having students grade their own work

- Having other teachers whose opinion we value observe our class presentation
- Helping students see the relevance of quality performance as it relates to future achievement in the job market

This last suggestion is interesting. **Most students do not experience the joy that comes from doing something well.** Motivation that comes from inside the child is more activating than external motivation. **When the value of intrinsic motivation is valued, the feeling of satisfaction becomes a guidepost for their future careers.** They also need to understand that people in the working world are financially rewarded for doing quality work.

9. **THE MATERIAL WE PRESENT MUST BE RELEVANT TO THE PRACTICAL NEEDS AND EXPERIENCE OF OUR STUDENTS.** Along with transmitting ideas, concepts and principles, teaching involves setting up challenges and conditions for children to make discoveries related to their physical and social environments. We need to shift our focus from grades and failing to solve a problem to considering and understanding the conditions that may affect learning such as: society's expectations, family and peer interactions.

Research has shown that we learn and retain:
    10% of what we hear
    15% of what we see
    20% of what we see and hear
    40% of what we discuss with others
    80% of what we experience directly and practice
    90% of what we attempt to teach others

10. **BECOMING A MASTERFUL TEACHER IS A PROCESS NOT AN EVENT.** To become good at anything requires experience and practice. Becoming a masterful teacher is no exception. For some of us, there is a tendency to beat ourselves up if we don't live up to our expectations

regarding our presentation. I often hear teachers say that they prepared the perfect lesson plan only to have it fall on deaf ears. **Our intention is to do what ever it takes in order to engage our students rather than focusing on being "right" about our degree of expertise.** It takes many years to manifest this level of skill and creativity. **We need to be patient with the process and learn to use our mistakes as an opportunity to learn rather than an opportunity to beat ourselves up.**

THE QUALITY TEACHER

1. OVER THE NEXT WEEK, CHOOSING ONE OF THE NINE AREAS DISCUSSED IN THIS CHAPTER, TAKE STEPS TO IMPROVE THE QUALITY OF YOUR TEACHING.

WHICH AREA DID YOU CHOOSE?

WHAT STEPS DID YOU TAKE?

119

WHAT WERE THE RESULTS OF YOUR ACTIONS?

2. IS THERE ANYTHING DIFFERENT AND EFFECTIVE THAT YOU DO IN YOUR CLASSROOM THAT MIGHT BENEFIT OTHER TEACHERS IN OUR CLASS?

PARTICIPANTS' COMMENTS

- A teacher shared, "A student of mine seemed very withdrawn, insecure and sad at the beginning of the semester. I knew that she was a foster child who had been coping with the confusion and difficulties of her situation. Her foster mother indicated to me that the child was a problem at home, yet I didn't experience her that way in school. I felt that it was important to affirm this child's positive attributes and to reward her efforts. I became her support — the person to whom she could turn for encouragement and to discuss her concerns. Recently, the foster mother told me how the child was doing better at home. I believe that, because of showing empathy and expressing interest in her, this student made and continues to make great progress."

- Another teacher shared, "I have a student who I thought had selective memory loss. It seemed the more I explained a set of directions, the more he claimed he didn't know what to do. Consequently, I stopped listening to him. My body language clearly reflected my displeasure with this student. I finally realized that he wanted my attention for himself and that this was his way of getting it. I now make a conscious effort to give this child extra attention. For example, having him check papers, calling on him for answers, etc. By choosing to respond to some of his needs, his attention demanding behavior has greatly subsided."

- A kindergarten teacher told about her experience with a student named Luis. "Luis was always withdrawn and angry. He was the only one in the class who couldn't tie his shoes, wash his hands, pour his own milk, clean himself or hold a fork. All the other children were very excited after I read a book entitled, *I Feel Good When I Learn New Things.* Suddenly, Luis started crying and said 'my mommy teach me nothing.' At that moment my whole perception changed. I felt bad because I realized that it wasn't his fault. It was simply that he had never been trained."

- Another educator commented, "When a student does a good job in school I make it my business to let the student know how proud I am of her. All too often educators find themselves reprimanding a student or dealing with their negative behavior. I try to 'catch them being good.' It is extremely important that we remember to say 'great job' or 'I'm proud of you' and other positive statements. I think this is a valuable way of building self-esteem."

- "I was very upset with a student who never brought home his report card and who never returned responses from notes that I sent home," shared another teacher. "I was very impatient with his excuses. When I changed my attitude, and began listening to him, I learned that he was being cared for by his sister. Both his parents worked nights and he almost never saw them. As a result of listening to him, I have asked the guidance counselor to investigate his case."

- A teacher reported, "I want to improve in area #1, 'students will rise to our level of expectation.' I usually start out with a high expectation during a lesson, but I am inconsistent in sustaining it during or after the lesson."

  "For example, on Monday my students had an essay due. We had worked on it in class the previous week. They were asked to write a final draft over the weekend. Most of the time, I get only one or two returned. This week, however, most of the students turned in their final drafts on time."

  "I had kept my expectation that all my students would turn in their essays. I had discussions with them about which question they were going to answer. I also spent individual time helping them to organize their thoughts. By the end of these conferences, most students had a clear idea of what they were going to write."

  "This time I did not give up on them. When three students did not hand their essays in on Monday, I agreed to accept their work on

Tuesday which resulted in all essays being turned in. It took a lot of effort to hold on to the intention that the students would take the work seriously, but happily, in the end that's exactly what they did."

- The following story from a high school teacher illustrates a creative way of encouraging quality work: "All semester, I had been tolerating the 'bare minimum' regarding my students' assignments. Last Thursday, I told them that I had a gift for everyone in the class. I proceeded to give each of them a crushed lollipop. I acted as if everything was alright. I asked them if they had any problems with the lollipops. They said that it seemed like I didn't care that I gave them left over candy from Halloween."

  "I then asked, 'How would you feel if someone gave you a shirt as a gift with a stain on it?' The general feeling was that they would be unhappy because it showed that the person did not care."

  "I continued, 'How do you think your teachers feel when you hand in assignments that are the bare minimum?' I went on to say that the assignments they hand in are a reflection of their caring for themselves. They understood. I then gave them a rubric which showed how I would grade their assignments."

  "It really worked. Although not all the students handed in the assignment, the work that was handed in demonstrated a lot of effort. Many of them created covers for their reports. One student even created a table of contents. Some asked for extra time to type it. They wanted to receive the best possible grade. This experience dramatically illustrated the role that I play in my students doing quality work."

- On positive discipline, one educator commented, "I'm really beginning to see the real individuals behind the adolescent armor which is making teaching a lot more rewarding and enjoyable."

- A high school science teacher shared, "Some weeks ago I stood in front of my students giving them definitions, formulae, etc. and trying to explain the concept of density. When it was time for evaluation I discovered that the students did not understand what I thought was the best lesson I had ever presented."

"Last week, as part of my assignment, I repeated the lesson without rigorous definitions, formulae or a lecture. This time the material presented was inquiry based — they did everything themselves and, most importantly everything that was presented was relevant to their practical needs and experience. I cannot remember a time when I was happier after giving a lesson."

- A teacher spoke about the reward system she instituted in her class: "Students accrue points (coupons) which are awarded for positive behavior and are traded in for items at the 'store.' The consequence for negative behavior is the loss of points (coupons). Various items have different trade-in values."

- Another teacher shared, "A strategy I used was to make Manuela my teaching assistant. I've given her many responsibilities which has totally transformed her disruptive behavior."

- Another teacher shared, "While having a conversation with Brit, a habitually disrespectful student, I mentioned that I was going to call her mother. She became angry, assuming that I had only bad news to report just like all the other teachers that had ever called. When I phoned, I did not discuss our combative encounters but, instead, spoke about how well Brit could work when she wanted to and. also, about how proud I was of her for the completion of her most recent project. I also asked her to inform Brit that I had called.

"The next day Brit, as usual, entered the class in her noisy and disruptive way. She settled down rather quickly. After class she came over and told me how surprised she was that I had something positive to report to her mother. I expressed that I really cared for her as my student, and that the only reason I spent so much time speaking to her is because she possessed talents that I knew needed to be brought forward.

EDUCATION FOR TRANSFORMATION

"Needless to say our relationship has dramatically improved and her class room behavior has become less disruptive as a result of my becoming less critical and more caring."

10

EMOTIONAL UNDERSTANDING

More than any other factor, a child's skill in managing his emotions will determine his level of achievement in life.

Dealing with children during times of emotional turmoil and conflict is one of the most stressful aspects of teaching. In this chapter, we will be presenting specific steps that will guide you through these potentially difficult times and help you to coach your students during emotional upheaval.

WHAT DO YOU DO WHEN A CHILD IS BLUE?

The very intention to teach is an act of love. However, loving and caring, although extremely important, are not enough; they are only the necessary first steps toward a fulfilling relationship with our students. With caring as our foundation, we have experienced increased growth as we have explored and become better at listening, taking responsibility, forgiving, accepting and communicating. But there is still another level of mastery that is necessary for success as an educator — knowing how to coach children when emotions run hot. Many people who are loving and caring have attitudes about their own as well as their children's emotions that prevent effective communication when a child is experiencing negative or tumultuous feelings.

According to researcher Dr. John Gotmen, there are two broad categories of people with regard to their response to emotional upset. People in one category give guidance and coaching in emotionally tumultuous situations. The others do not. The first group, whom Gotmen calls emotion coaches, view feelings such as fear, anger and sadness as opportunities for children to learn valuable life lessons. They are able to accept children's feelings and patiently help them to find creative solutions to their problems. Further on in the chapter, we will discuss emotion coaching in greater depth. Now let's discuss the group who choose not to provide guidance and support when children are experiencing negative emotions.

The Dismissive Adult wants to make the world perfect and believes that children are never supposed to be sad. They pamper them and don't acknowledge or discuss negative emotions such as fear and anger. They often don't show their own emotions because they are afraid that their own anger might devastate someone. Instead of empathizing with children's emotional outbursts, they refer to them as cute.

The Disapproving Adult is often critical and lacks empathy for children's negative emotions. They regard anger or crying as a form of manipulation. Obedience is their main concern. These individuals often punish a boy for expressing fear or require a girl to swallow her anger.

The Laissez-Faire Adult is similar to the emotion coach in that they accept all feelings. The difference lies in their inability to give guidance while a child is experiencing negative or turbulent emotions. These are the overly permissive teachers who often do not set adequate boundaries for their students.

THE EMOTION COACH

Emotion coaches, according to Gotman, guide and counsel children toward solutions to their problems. They don't try to "fix" everything but instead focus on the potential for learning from the experiences that emotional storms can provide. They value being real and are not afraid to apologize when they handle a situation poorly. They show emotions in front of their children. They are aware that children can learn about the staying power of relationships by observing arguments and then seeing them resolved. These parents set limits and relate consequences to actions. Research has shown that children of these Parental Masters:

- Get along better with, show more affection to, and feel less tension around their parents
- Are less prone to becoming upset, and when they do become upset, recover more quickly
- Are more relaxed as indicated by lower levels of stress hormones
- Are more popular with their peers and more highly regarded by their teachers
- Are more attentive and learn more effectively
- Have higher achievement scores in math and reading by the time they reach the third grade

These children exemplify positive attributes not because of obedience and forced compliance but because they feel connected to their parents through empathy and understanding.

If we multiply these results, we can see how transformation will occur on a significant societal level as more children are coached by masterful parents and teachers. These are adults who demonstrate forgiveness, acceptance, reflection and responsibility in their lives, while relating to their children in a compassionate, trusting and loving way. This is not a fantasy, but a reality that can occur through education, training, practice and will.

The five basic steps for emotion coaching apply the wisdom gained from the previous chapters.

1. **THE FIRST STEP IS TO BECOME CLEAR ABOUT OUR INTENTION.** The intention of an emotion coach is to use the child's emotional outburst as an opportunity for guidance and intimacy. This is a very different intention from using the display of negative emotions as an opportunity to make the child wrong, deny his experience or punish him. Getting clear about our intention in any situation goes a long way to fulfilling our desires.

2. **NEXT, WE BECOME AWARE OF WHICH SPECIFIC EMOTIONS WE**

ARE EXPERIENCING. Once we acknowledge what we are feeling, we need to take responsibilityfor how we feel. I demonstrate this in class by asking one of the participants to call me a liar. We then discuss the various responses I could choose, such as calmly stating, "I am not a liar" or angrily threatening, "Who are you calling a liar?" or "I may have lied in the past but I'm not lying now." Who determines my response to being called a liar? I do. **Our students don't make us angry, upset or sad. We are the source of what we feel.**

3. **WE LISTEN WITH AN EMPATHETIC HEART.** This is the most important quality of an emotion coach. As we feel what the other is feeling, we become our student's ally. For this to happen, we must listen and do nothing else. We must be able to hear, accept and not want to change what the child is feeling. We must embrace the child's sadness, whininess, anger, crying, impatience, disappointment and frustration. Not an easy task, but remember we are talking about Mastery here.

4. **NEXT, WE ASSIST THE CHILD TO VERBALLY LABEL AND COMMUNICATE THE EMOTIONS SHE IS FEELING.** By prompting with questions, we help the child to verbalize her emotional state (e.g. I feel angry, sad, bored, tired, etc.) Of course, the response depends on the child's age, but I have heard very young children give articulate answers when encouraged to describe their feelings.

5. **WE RECOGNIZE AND ACKNOWLEDGE THE CHILD'S UNFULFILLED NEEDS.** Often, we become emotional upset when our need for love, joy, safety, appreciation, freedom or cooperation is not being met. Conflicts often arise when a child's need for freedom, independence or self expression challenges our need for their safety and order in the classroom.

Communication that acknowledges both party's needs and feelings, rather than negatively judging our own as well as the student's needs, goes a long way towards peaceful resolving these types of situations. Shouting, "I can't take this anymore. How many times do I have to tell you to be quiet," is one way of communicating your displeasure. Another way, which honors needs and choice, is stating, "I recognize your need to talk and share ideas. I have the need to communicate information in a quiet classroom. How can we satisfy both our needs?" This way of communicating honors our needs and also teaches our students to honor and express their needs.

6. **FINALLY, WE SUPPORT THE CHILD IN HER ATTEMPT TO FIND A SOLUTION TO HER PROBLEMS.** This process begins with asking what she thinks would be the best solution. Then we go on to discuss alternative solutions. Questions such as: "How would you feel if you were in his place?" "What have been the consequences when you have acted that way?" and "What can you do to best serve yourself and the other people involved?" go a long way to bringing peace and fulfillment back into the child's life. We must always keep in mind that as teachers we must set limits. Students need to realize that all emotions — but not all behaviors — are acceptable. After a consideration of all the consequences of each choice, we can encourage the child to pick one solution.

AGAIN, WE TEACH WHO WE ARE

The six steps of emotion coaching can only be effective in the hands of teachers who are skillful in managing their own feelings. Once again, the emphasis is, "we teach who we are."

The root of the inability to establish an empathetic connection can be found in our own upbringing. If our parents were not emotion coaches how could we to learn how to manage our feelings? If our parents were afraid of or not in control of their own emotions, then emotions may seem as threatening to us as they were to them. However, we owe it to ourselves and our students to explore other more beneficial ways of managing our feelings. By being open enough to consider the possibility of becoming an emotion coach, you have come a long way already. We must be patient with ourselves in acquiring the skills we need in order to be the teacher our students deserve.

Our emotional health is determined mainly by the quality of the intimate relationships that surround us. When parents nurture and support one another, the child's ability to resolve upset is greatly enhanced. Research has shown that children living in environments where parents are critical, hostile and show contempt for each other are likely to have problems managing their own emotions, tend to be aggressive and have more problems getting along with others. Even divorce in itself is not as detrimental to a child's well being as is the way couples relate to each other while they are together or after a divorce. Research has also shown that, especially for children of color, the caring and quality of relationship that a teacher develops with their students, is more important in the overall learning process when compared with a teachers method of presentation and knowledge of the subject being presented.

Although this chapter focuses on our interaction with our students, the steps for managing emotional upset and resolving conflict are also meant to be used internally and with any appropriate person in our lives. Using every opportunity available to make us a more conscious human being will make us more masterful teachers.

The next homework assignment is to be done over a three-week period. Its purpose is to demonstrate the power that intention, taking responsibility and taking action have as agents of transformation in our lives.

THE RELATIONSHIP PROJECT

1. FOR THE NEXT THREE WEEKS, WHO DO YOU WANT TO FOCUS ON AND WORK TOWARD IMPROVING YOUR RELATIONSHIP WITH?

131

2. LIST SPECIFIC AREAS THAT YOU WOULD LIKE TO IMPROVE.

3. WRITE ABOUT THE EFFECTS OF THE STEPS OR INTERVENTIONS YOU TOOK TO IMPROVE YOUR RELATIONSHIP WITH THE PERSON YOU CHOSE.   EDUCATION FOR TRANSFORMATION

Examples of outer interventions:

- Writing a letter to the person
- Taking them out to dinner, a movie, etc. Giving them something that shows you care
- Communicating lovingly once a day
- Telling them how much you appreciate them, i.e. GRATITUDE
- Clearing up areas of your life that are incomplete with them i.e. COMMUNICATION
- Observing patterns of communication that may not serve your relationship (e.g. aggressive or passive behavior) and making changes

Examples of inner interventions:

- Getting in touch with and forgiving yourself for any judgment you have against the other person (do this at least three times a day)
- Thinking of them lovingly — see the person with a smile on their face everyday
- At least once a day, visualize what it would look like to have a good relationship with this person

4. RECORD WHAT CHANGES YOU OBSERVED IN YOUR RELATION-SHIP WHEN YOU TOOK INTERNAL ACTIONS BASED ON PRINCI-PLES EXPLORED IN THIS BOOK:

- TAKING RESPONSIBILITY
- ACCEPTANCE
- CHOICE
- FORGIVENESS

133

5. RATE FROM 1-10 YOUR LEVEL OF SATISFACTION WITH YOUR RELATIONSHIP BEFORE DOING THE ASSIGNMENT AND AGAIN AFTER ITS COMPLETION.

6. WHAT SPECIFIC LESSONS HAVE YOU INCORPORATED INTO YOUR RELATIONSHIP WITH YOUR CHILDREN? STUDENTS? FRIENDS? RELATIVES?

134

11

PRACTICING POSITIVE DISCIPLINE THROUGH THE UNDERSTANDING OF OUR STUDENTS' TEMPERAMENTS

The more awareness and empathy we bring to understanding our students' behavior, the better able we are to guide them in a positive direction.

A person's temperament is not the same as his or her personality. It is but one part of the personality along with intelligence, emotion and sense of humor. Temperament is the distinguishing style or characteristic that makes someone's personality unique. It is normal for each individual to bring a distinct set of behavior patterns to various situations. These patterns are a reflection of that person's temperament.

Approximately half a child's temperament is inherited, explains William B. Carey, M.D., in his book *Understanding Your Child's Temperament.* The other half is determined by a combination of physical, psychological and environmental factors such as conditions during the mother's pregnancy (e.g., nutrition, drug use or general health); the child's physical health after birth and the influence of the family. Teachers need to recognize the inborn nature of temperament since many problems in classroom management come from trying to work against and change the child's natural behavioral style. **We cannot change a child's basic temperament. But we can alter and control the way we respond to and manage it.** This is where the principles of acceptance and how you relate to the issue is issue come into play. Given that a child's temperament is basically pre-determined, how you relate to and accept that temperament can either support or disrupt the interaction you have with that child. **In essence, how you feel about and adapt to a student's temperament is as important as the temperament itself.**

Dr. Carey describes nine traits that blend together to determine a

135

child's unique, largely inborn temperament. Understanding these traits can help you to become more accepting of each child's individuality. Ideally, you should observe them in various settings at different times. For instance when observing the "activity" trait, look for fidgeting while eating, reading, watching TV and standing on line..

ACTIVITY

This characteristic refers to physical motion during sleep, play, work, eating, dressing, bathing and other daily activities. Does the student usually sit still or squirm around and fidget? The tendency to be more active and engaged in one's surroundings should not be confused with hyperactivity which tends to be disorganized and without purpose.

REGULARITY

This trait determines how predictable a child's responses will be to the events in his or her daily life. For young children, it can be observed in their cycle of sleeping, eating and elimination. In older children this trait manifests itself in behavior such as completing tasks on schedule.

INITIAL REACTION

This is how a child initially responds to new people, situations, places, food, toys and procedures. At one end of the spectrum is the child who accepts and approaches ordinary degrees of novelty with little hesitation and adapts quickly. At the other end is the shy, timid child who does not engage in new situations or withdraws from them entirely, at least for a while.

ADAPTABILITY

Adaptability is the adjustment over the long term that follows the initial response. It shows a range between flexibility and rigidity in adjusting to the environment after the child's first reaction. For instance, notice how quickly a specific student adapts when his or her seat assignment is changed.

INTENSITY

Intensity is the measure of how much energy a child puts into his or her responses, regardless of whether the response is positive and happy or negative and fussy. A more intense child will be more physically active and louder in his or her responses while a placid child will show less expression of feeling and physical motion.

MOOD

A child's predominant mood can be positive, negative, or somewhere in between. To better assess a child's predisposition for mood, look for an overall pattern that occurs in various situations.

PERSISTENCE AND ATTENTION SPAN

Persistence refers to a child's inclination to stick with an activity despite obstacles or interruptions. Attention span is demonstrated by how long a child continues an activity or pursues a task when there are no interruptions.

137

DISTRACTIBILITY

Some children are easily distracted by noise, light, sounds or other people, whereas other children have no problem tuning out stimuli and continuing a task without interruption. A child's level of distractibility does not necessarily affect his or her persistence because a child can be very easily distracted yet still return immediately to a task and stick with it until is finished.

SENSITIVITY

Sensitivity refers to the amount of stimulation from factors such as noise, sights, smells and lights needed to rouse a response. All five senses give clues to the child's sensitivity trait.

Some of these categories tend to cluster together. For instance, many shy children have a slow initial response, are less adaptable, have lower intensity of response, are less physically active and experience more negative moods. Similarly, the "easy" cluster of traits describes children who are pleasant, flexible, not too intense and fairly predictable.

Also, be aware that the child's age can affect the constancy of the temperament he or she exhibits. During adolescence factors such as hormones, dietary eccentricities sleep deprivation, rigorous athletic training and the use of drugs or alcohol can influence a teenager's temperament. Also, by this age youngsters can alter their temperaments to "fit" with their peers. For instance, a youth may push himself forward in spite of feeling timid and having a shy temperament. Although the expression may be different, the feelings are still there.

TEMPERAMENT AND STRESS

In school age children, the traits that influence development the most strongly are persistence, attention span and adaptability. In fact, a child's temperament seems to contribute more to test results than I.Q. For example, teachers' ratings of high attention span high persistence, low distractibility and low activity among elementary school students were shown to relate to better performance on standardized achievement tests in reading and mathematics. Likewise, the traits of low persistence, high distractibility, high activity, shyness low adaptability and negative mood often contributed to poorer classroom performance.

Research has shown that eight of the nine more challenging traits were significantly associated with the development of stress: high activity, low adaptability, withdrawal from new stimuli, distractibility, high intensity, negative mood, low persistence and irregularity. A study of 155 normal six- to nine-year-old children found a correlation between high levels of stress and behavioral problems. For example, children with low adaptability and high intensity are much less likely to adjust to a newborn sibling or the divorce of their parents and will as a result experience elevated levels of stress as a result.

ADAPTING TO YOUR STUDENT'S TEMPERAMENT

How you react to a student's temperament not only affects the student-teacher interaction but also can have a positive or negative impact on your personal relationships, work performance, self-assurance and various aspects of mental and bodily functions, such as eating and sleeping. It affects our self-esteem and our competence as teachers when we allow our inability to accept and cope to produce frustration, anger and guilt. Our student's positive temperament traits can make us feel successful as teachers, whereas having to deal with a difficult child can make us feel ineffective.

Some children are just harder to relate to. It's much easier to teach a child who easily accepts and adapts to new things whereas a child with a more resistant temperament can frustrate even the calmest teacher leaving them stressed and feeling incompetent. Similarly, intense, high-spirited, persistent children can be exhausting to supervise. And a child who is stubborn, who frowns, sulks and protests and is abrasive is much harder to be warm to than a child who is friendly, upbeat, pays attention to requests and rarely complains.

We need to observe the impact that a child's temperament has on you. Which traits please you, bother you and cause friction? For example, a very active child may delight a phys ed teacher but totally unnerve a physics teacher who leads a quiet, sedentary life. Gender can also affect how we relate to a trait. Shyness is traditionally more acceptable in girls than in boys whereas high activity is usually not as well accepted in girls as it is in boys. Certain traits may be easier to accept in one phase of a child's development but deemed negative in another. For instance, a young child who adapts easily to new people and environments is regarded with a great deal of acceptance. However, this same trait in adolescence can lead to experimentation with drugs, alcohol, tobacco and other types of risky behavior.

The chart on the following pages from Dr. Carey's book *Understanding Your Child's Temperament* illustrates the positive and negative aspects of different character traits and how they can affect the teacher-child relationship.

139

TRAIT	SOMETIME NEGATIVE ASPECTS	GENERALLY POSITIVE ASPECTS
Activity	**High:** Social activities and task performance are easily interfered with. May be mislabeled "hyperactive." Hyperactivity is disorganized, purposeless activity and not simply high activity. **Low:** Slow to perform tasks; may seem drowsy; may be labeled "lazy."	**High:** Vigorous and energetic; explores surroundings; stays active in dull environments. **Low:** Less disruptive in cramped environments and circumstances.
Regularity	**High:** May be a problem if the environment cannot provide for needs on schedule. **Low:** Unpredictable care requirements.	**High:** Few surprises for parents and other caregivers. **Low:** May not be bothered by irregularities in caregiving or routine events.
Initial reaction	**Approaching or bold:** May accept negative influences too quickly, which is dangerous in hazardous environments. **Withdrawing or inhibited:** Slow to accept change; may avoid useful experiences.	**Approaching or bold:** Makes a rapid fit in favorable settings. **Withdrawing or inhibited:** Cautious in dangerous situations e.g. in accepting offers from strangers.
Adaptability	**High:** In danger of accepting negative influences, such as antisocial values of peers. **Low:** May have difficulty adjusting to requirements of caregiving; stress-producing; may be labeled "difficult."	**High:** Generally at an advantage; accepts positive influences more quickly; in greater harmony with caregivers. **Low:** Less likely to accept negative influences.

140

TRAIT	SOMETIME NEGATIVE ASPECTS	GENERALLY POSITIVE ASPECTS
Intensity	**High:** Abrasive and annoying; may evoke counterintensity; may mislead parents or other caregivers as to seriousness of an issue or illness. **Low:** Needs may not be expressed with enough forcefulness to be recognized.	**High:** Needs are certain to get attention; caregivers welcome the positive intensity. **Low:** Easier to live with.
Mood	**Positive:** May be too positive and upbeat about real problems. **Negative:** Unpleasant for parents and other caregivers, who may overestimate importance of issue or physical complaint.	**Positive:** Welcome. **Negative:** Few advantages; however, may evoke more positive involvement from parents and other caregivers because of their concerns.
Persistence and attention span	**High:** Being absorbed in work and play may make the child seem to ignore parents, teachers, etc. **Low:** Less efficient at task performances; fails to perform as expected. Not to be considered an "attention-deficit" if the child functions well, particularly in combination with compensatory factors such as high adaptability and intelligence.	**High:** Greater achievement likely at various tasks and school performance. **Low:** May be more easily drawn out of activities or habits that are unacceptable to parents and other caregivers.
Distractibility	**High:** Easily diverted from tasks; performance is easily interfered with; needs reminders. **Low:** May be unaware of important signals, such as warnings from parents.	**High:** Easy to soothe as an infant. **Low:** Can work efficiently in noisy places.

141

TRAIT	SOMETIME NEGATIVE ASPECTS	GENERALLY POSITIVE ASPECTS
Sensitivity	**High:** More perceptive of surrounding noises, smells, lights, textures, and internal sensations; as an infant, more prone to colic and sleep disturbances. **Low:** May miss important cues from surroundings.	**High:** More aware of changes in environment and of existence and nuances of other peoples' thoughts and feelings. **Low:** More shielded from too much environmental input.

From William B. Carey, M.D. *Understanding Your Child's Temperament*, New York: MacMillan, 1997: pp. 53-56.

142 You cannot change a child's temperament. You cannot hammer the undesirable traits out of a student with rigid discipline. What you can do is learn to accept those traits, and at the same time develop alternative ways to manage a child's temperament to reduce stress and maximize harmonious interaction.

PRACTICAL SUGGESTIONS FOR EFFECTIVELY MANAGING
SPECIFIC TRAITS

ACTIVITY

Active children need outlets for their energy and the opportunity for physical motion while also needing to be taught about boundaries. For example, taking timed breaks during lessons to allow students to get up and stretch or move around.

By contrast, children who are low in activity need more time to complete tasks. They are often judged as "lazy" and do not perform well on standardized tests. Sometimes we can speed up these children without criticizing them. For instance they could be given a kitchen timer or hourglass as a way of keeping them in touch with a time requirement.

REGULARITY

Children high in regularity are very predictable and have no problem following routine schedules but they can become very upset if schedules are changed at the last minute. A way to deal with this is to give as much advance notice as possible before making changes. Also, being very loving and nurturing when explaining changes to routine scheduling is a way of respecting this trait and encouraging more adaptability in the future.

Children with a low regularity trait have trouble keeping to schedules. They should also be complimented and/or rewarded for being early or on time in various situations. These types of children would do best in a day care center or school with a loosely organized schedule.

Of course, temperament is not an excuse for the adolescent who is chronically late for class because they are rebellious or just looking for attention. There is a fine line between inborn temperament and manipulation through certain types of behavior.

INITIAL REACTION

Entering unfamiliar territory is easy for children whose initial reaction is positive or outgoing. They enjoy meeting new people and exploring new places. These children should be told that it is good to be friendly, but to be wary of strangers. Younger children should be constantly told not to go with anyone they don't know.

On the other hand, teachers should not punish a child whose initial response to novelty is withdrawal. Offering gentle encouragement and preparing them for a new experience in advance is usually more effective than coercion or forced compliance.

ADAPTABILITY

The flexibility that a child displays in accepting change should not be taken for granted but encouraged as often as possible. The only downside to a high level of adaptability can be a willingness to embody negative ideas and concepts from peers, the internet or television. We should be cautious and monitor their child's exposure to possible negative influences.

Children with low adaptability usually just require extra time, preparation or advance warning in order to adjust. For example, if you are planning a field trip, you can show your students pictures and answer any of their questions beforehand.

INTENSITY

Children with high intensity seem to operate consistently at a higher volume. Their loud, dramatic, responses don't always mean that their position is emotionally charged or that they're unwilling to compromise. It's just their way of communicating. With these youngsters, teachers are better off responding in a composed, even and understanding tone rather than trying to match the child's level of intensity.

With a low intensity child we need to realize that feelings and thoughts expressed unemotionally in a low voice may be as important as those expressed loudly by more intense children. For example, the child may be experiencing strong physical discomfort caused by an illness but never utter a word whereas the high intensity child might cry and scream, causing you to send them to the school nurse for a problem that does not warrant such treatment.

MOOD

Some children simply don't come into this life with sunny dispositions. Teachers can help children reduce a tendency toward negativity by giving them nurturing suggestions, such as, "Johnny might respond more nicely to you if you went out of your way and were nice to him first." Being patient and not trying to constantly persuade the child to cheer up are keys to helping the child see the world in a brighter light.

PERSISTENCE AND ATTENTION SPAN

Children who manifest a low persistence trait tend to falter before finishing things. They are less likely to follow through on homework and classroom tasks. Dividing long tasks into smaller segments with breaks in between can help less persistent or attentive children complete their assignments.

DISTRACTIBILITY

For adolescents, a tendency toward becoming distracted can be disruptive and unproductive. These children should not be allowed to have the television or radio on while they are doing homework and should have a quiet room where they can study without interruption. Also, when having a discussion with a child who loses focus easily, it is wise to do so in a place that is quiet and free from distractions. On the other hand, there are some adolescents who can actually study better and retain more information listening to music or the television while doing their homework.

SENSITIVITY

Highly sensitive children are more aware of and more reactive to changes in their environment. These children can irritate others with their heightened sensitivity but in reality they are simply more attuned to what is going on around them. Teachers should avoid placing negative labels such as "finicky," "complainer" or "difficult" on these children.

TEMPERAMENT AND BEHAVIORAL PROBLEMS

Temperament can be a cause of behavioral problems when it conflicts with our values and expectations. Researchers found that when adults responded poorly to the "difficult" trait cluster of low adaptability, withdrawing initial reaction, negative mood, high intensity and irregularity, the child often responded by behaving in an inappropriate fashion. Ask yourself: Could pushing a shy child too hard be the cause of his resistance to interact with classmates? Could a child's rebellion against the new second-grade teacher stem from the instructor's demands that all children adjust to her rigid program? Could a child's constant acting out in class be due to the lack of physical movement and exercise allowed by her teacher? Could badgering a child to be more upbeat contribute to her not wanting to go anywhere with the rest of the class? Could imposing a rigid time schedule on a child be causing her to rebel by never being on time?

It is not the "difficult" traits themselves that cause the problem, rather, it is the way that some teachers responds to these traits. Many parents and teachers have a problem dealing with the spontaneous, inquisitive and rambunctious nature of many of today's youth. In many instances, behavioral problems are a result of adults not respecting and honoring children's perceptions and points of view but, instead taking the attitude of "my way or the highway". I'm not suggesting that you surrender your authority — I'm asking you to be creative and look for alternative approaches that take a child's temperament into consideration to reach the same goal. Work with a child's temperament, not against it.

Similarly, children with learning disabilities have normal temperaments just like children without learning disabilities - the behavioral problems often occur when teachers do not alter their interaction to produce a better "fit" with the traits and temperaments of these children. Many adolescents diagnosed with ADHD are exhibiting normal temperaments that are "difficult" to deal with. The three major components of ADHD — distractibility, impulsiveness, and restlessness — are all symptoms of a neurological problem that causes a decreased blood flow to the frontal area of the brain. It is a disability that can be detected clinically utilizing a SPECT profile (a radiographic technique used to measure blood flow to the prefrontal area of the brain). Very few children who have been labeled ADHD have had a SPECT profile to confirm their diagnosis. The ADHD diagnosis often fails to recognize that half of normal children are more active, more inattentive or more distractible than average.

Dr. Russell Barkley, Ph.D., author of *Taking Charge of ADHD: The Complete Authoritative Guide for Parents*, states that the common problem with adolescents diagnosed with ADHD is self-regulation or a low adaptability temperament. **Do the 10 percent of children today who are being diagnosed as ADHD really all have brain abnormalities or is the diagnosis in part a reflection of society's inability to deal with the temperament traits of low adaptability, low attentiveness, high distractibility, and high activity?**

Classroom management is the main challenge whether a student has been correctly diagnosed with ADHD or is just extremely difficult to deal with because of his low adaptability, low attentiveness, high distractibility, and high activity. Here are several suggestions for managing these "difficult" students:

- Seat the child near the teacher's desk. Traditional seating with the difficult student in the first row is preferable to modular seating with several students seated at a large table. Also traditional classrooms are preferable to the open classrooms.

- Activities should be broken up into small segments letting the child take more frequent breaks. Students may need longer breaks just before times of diminished alertness such as during the period before recess, just before lunch or midway between lunch and dismissal.

- Create a log of when students are more or less alert during the day as a guide for presenting lessons that require more cognition. In general, difficult work should be scheduled in the morning rather than at the end of the day.

- The volume of presentation should be adjusted to take into consideration the student's ability to concentrate. In general, the length of an assignment should be given as if the student were 30 percent younger.

- There should be periods of quiet time during the day where students can rest, play quiet games or explore their learning strengths.

- Everything possible should be done in creating a lesson plan to engage and hold the interest of these children. A variety of modalities such as: drawings, role-play, films, audio tapes, collaborative lessons and learning in small groups can be employed. Repeatedly asking questions can also keep students more involved.

- Keep these children involved and active. Cleaning the blackboard or helping in collecting or passing out materials are ways to maintain focus. Physical activity or movement such as squeezing a tennis ball, tapping a pencil on their leg, doodling during a presentation or raising their hands in response to a question should be encouraged.

- These students often have difficulty filtering out distractions and detecting which stimuli are important to focus on. They may often feel overwhelmed or overloaded in school. The use of different colors to emphasize certain points, eye contact, graphs, outlines and background white noise can help students focus. Specific audio tapes produced by the Monroe institute in Virginia have been created to stimulate the attention arousal portion of the brain.

- In general, these students respond poorly to pressure. The best form of motivation is praise and encouragement rather than pressure.

- They often seek conflict because it gives them an adrenalin rush, which increases blood flow to the frontal portion of the brain. Try to avoid conflict and confrontation. Brief, business-like, non-emotional reprimands that are backed up with consequences seem to work best. Punishment that involves the removal of rewards or privileges is preferred to the use of aversive events such as isolation.

- Send home a form that evaluates the child's behavior each day. The parent can use this feedback to reinforce good behavior.

- Avoid comments such as, "You're not trying. I know you can do this because I've seen you do this before," with students who have inconsistent mental effort control. Although teachers and parents are often confused by this inconsistency and unreliability, it is worth noting that the students themselves are often as confused by these inconsistencies.

- There may be a problem with self-monitoring, which is the ongoing feedback regarding the quality of one's performance. Students with this problem are apt to make frequent careless errors while writing, doing math, detecting social cues, etc. Assistance can come in the form of:
Using checklists

Delaying quality control for 24 hours after completion of assignment

Providing examples of quality work

Interspersing questions during a lesson instead of having all the questions only at the end

Writing down a summary of something just read

Self-grading and evaluation

- Many of these students have poor previewing control. This may result in a lack of foresight and an inability to estimate outcomes in areas such as math, reading, listening to stories, or planning elements of projects. It can be helpful to display models of desired outcomes and past work done by other students, and to provide checklists of steps and goals.

  This tendency to do the first thing that comes to mind without considering consequences or other possibilities often manifests in problems in verbal or vocal control, behavior or emotive control, and hyperactivity. Offer different strategies that a student may incorporate in many various situations. Present from the point of view of choices and consequences for those choices. Encourage students to stop and pause for five seconds before responding verbally to any question. Teach and stress "problem solving techniques". Give exercises that emphasize reflection and that resolve questions, such as: "Would I do the same thing again? What part of the plan would I change?"

- Help them find careers that suit their temperaments and offer stimulation by considering factors such as: multiple environments, various responsibilities, independence, the ability to work at own pace without the constant scrutiny of others, and the freedom to move around.

NOW FOR THE GOOD NEWS

Due to their high level of creativity and intelligence, many children who manifested the behavioral traits of low adaptability, poor concentration, restlessness and hyperactivity have gone on to become very successful adults. These individuals have been able to channel the traits that were negatively judged when they were growing up into strengths during adulthood. They have learned to focus their high energy so they can get more done in one day. Their high creativity coupled with a strong intuitive sense often produces original thinkers who are more independent, sensitive, and compassionate. Because they are very impulsive and non-reflective they can be very passionate and emotional about their actions and as a result, do things with more personal conviction than most people. In that they are creatures of the moment, they are more apt to take chances and thus often lead more exciting lives as a result.

Remembering the gifts of these so called "learning disabled" children can go a long way to helping us have compassion and hope and feel less frustration in our daily interactions with them. Here is a partial list of "learning disabled" youngsters who have significantly contributed to humanity.

Pablo Picasso
Leonardo da Vinci
Winston Churchill
Greg Louganis
Bruce Jenner
Cher
Woodrow Wilson
Thomas Edison
Abraham Lincoln
Alexander Graham Bell
Benjamin Franklin
Henry David Thoreau

PRACTICING POSITIVE DISCIPLINE

With the understanding of temperament as a foundation, we are now able to approach discipline in a more compassionate and understanding manner. One of the most important things a teacher can do to manage a child with a difficult temperament is to simply listen. Taking a moment to reflect before responding to a child rather than acting on impulse is another way of letting your student know that you really care. Both strategies show a concerted effort on your part to understand the child's point of view.

In his book *Taking Charge of ADHD: The Complete Authoritative Guide for Parents*, author Russell A. Barkley, Ph.D. offers several techniques for dealing with ADHD which are also applicable to difficult children and those with strong temperamental qualities:

POSITIVE REINFORCEMENT

Rewarding children for good behavior and fining them for overstepping boundaries can be a very effective way to establish new behavior patterns. **Difficult children require more powerful positive consequences than children with easier temperaments.** Depending on the child's age you may want to reward good behavior with tokens or special privileges. For instance, always being to school on time, doing exemplary homework, or always lining up quietly can be rewarded with five tokens whereas putting crayons away, not fighting with others, and hanging up coats can be rewarded with 2 tokens. Similarly, you can fine a child for not obeying established guidelines or following through on promises. But be careful about using too many fines — **you should focus more on rewarding positive behavior than penalizing a child for stepping out of bounds.** Also (if using a token system) be sure to determine the value of the tokens so the child knows what they are worth. For example, watching a film in class for 15 minutes could be worth five tokens while special rewards like going on a field trip could be worth 200 tokens.

WORK BEFORE FUN

A similar strategy, called the Primack principle, is to deny a child access to more enjoyable activities until the less-fun or necessary work is done. For example, telling your class that they can go to the playground only after all the crayons are picked up from the floor. This turns ordinarily accessible activities into privileges that must be earned.

MANAGING ATTENTION SPAN

Because temperamental children (children with difficult temperaments) often have shorter attention spans and are more easily distracted, it can help to split homework into more manageable segments. Helpful suggestions to parents regarding these children include:

- Do 15 minutes of homework when he or she comes home, 15 minutes before dinner, and 15 minutes after dinner.
- Do homework in areas of the house that work best for the child's study habits.
- Have them take frequent breaks or vary activities. Music could either help or hinder the child's ability to concentrate.
- Ask the parents to see if certain foods affect the child's ability to concentrate. Pay special attention to allergens, such as preservatives, wheat, dairy and sugar.

153

FREQUENT FEEDBACK

Frequent feedback, especially positive feedback, is far more effective than punishment with temperamental children. Use punishment only after frequent feedback and incentives fail to change negative behavior.

TIME OUTS

Calling "time out" can be a good strategy if a young child does not respond to two repeated requests. State your request firmly but not angrily. **A time out should not be viewed as punishment, but instead as a break taken by you and a child in order to restore a more balanced and**

loving interaction. If she does not respond or says "no," wait five seconds and repeat the request. If she doesn't obey, tell her that she will have to sit in a chair for a minimum of two minutes. (A good time formula is to penalize the child with a minimum of one or two minutes for each year of age.) Wait another five seconds. Then if she refuses to comply, send her to the time out. Once the minimum sentence is over, wait for her to be quiet for 30 seconds. Now she must agree to comply with your original request, or apologize if she said something mean or inappropriate. As soon as she agrees, be sure to give praise for the cooperation. If she still refuses to comply, use the time out strategy again.

FAIR PLAY

Teachers should take special care to teach a difficult child how to play with other children in a positive, non-aggressive fashion. Talk about and define specific behaviors that are desirable as well as those that aren't appreciated when relating to classmates. While the child is interacting with his peers constantly remind him of the desired behavior and offer positive reinforcement when he acts appropriately. Other helpful strategies are to discourage competition and not allow out of control friends to play together. But beyond all techniques, the most powerful influence on a child's interaction with his or her peers is the type of behavior you model in your classroom.

PREPARATION

If you know that a student usually demonstrates negative behavior in certain situations, prepare in advance to reduce the likelihood of a disagreement. For instance, before breaking the class into smaller groups for an assignment, talk to the student about the type of behavior you expect, along with the punishment or rewards that he can expect depending upon his behavior. Temperamental children respond poorly to pressure. The best form of motivation is praise and encouragement rather than pressure in the heat of the moment.

CLEAR COMMUNICATION

Instead of asking a question, present commands in a direct fashion. For example, "Please pick up that pen," is far more effective than "Do you want to pick up that pen?" After giving the command, give immediate feedback based on the student's response. For example, if the child does not respond to your request, restate the command and be prepared to ask for a time out. Similarly, if the child obeys, be sure to say thank you and show your appreciation.

ADVANCE NOTICE

Many children have a problem switching from a fun activity such as play to one they perceive to be boring such as writing or science. A few minutes before the transition, give the class advance notice. Have them repeat what you have just said so you are clear they understand. When the time comes for the transition, give the command in an assertive but emotionally neutral fashion. Don't engage in an argument if certain children protest but, instead, use the punishment-reward system and/or time out if necessary.

CREDIBILITY

This means that if you say there will be consequences or you will not tolerate a certain type of behavior then stick to your guns, be firm and don't give in.

AN UNDERSTANDING TEACHER

The compassion, understanding and commitment to the child's well-being that a teacher demonstrates can be the single most important variable regarding the success of difficult or temperamental students.

PATIENCE AND FORGIVENESS

Many difficult children cause conflict within the class because of their constant need for stimulation. It is extremely important to keep cool rather than to invite strife and discord. Similarly, you must constantly remember that you are dealing with a difficult temperament and practice forgiveness each day for their behavior, your behavior and other judgments others may have.

TAKE CARE OF YOURSELF SO YOU CAN TAKE CARE OF OTHERS

Teachers of difficult children often experience significantly higher levels of stress, depression and self-blame than teachers who have "easier" children. You can reduce your level of stress by practicing relaxation techniques, engaging in exercise, pursuing a hobby, listening to music, becoming active in support groups, taking vacations, educating yourself regarding the nature and cause of specific disabilities and by being aware of what you eat and how it affects you. Reread Chapter 3 on Taking Care of Yourself for further suggestions.

Most importantly, give frequent positive feedback when your students demonstrate positive behavior.

DEALING WITH A TEMPERAMENTAL TEEN

Dealing with temperamentally difficult teenagers can be especially trying. In her book **Why Teens Are So Critical**, Kathleen McCoy, Ph.D. explains that it's perfectly normal for children to become more difficult and temperamental during their teen years, and that this phase is just part of the maturation process.

Adolescence generally happens between the ages of eleven and nineteen, during which time a child will undergo several important biological and psychological changes. Throughout this period, children will:

- MATURE PHYSICALLY
- MATURE SEXUALLY
- DEFINE VALUES
- MANIFEST PERSONAL POWER
- INDIVIDUATE

157

They will also be dealing with all sorts of new concerns such as physical appearance, the opinions of their peers, wanting to belong, drugs and music.

Dr. McCoy states that the child is working towards one of the major goals of adolescence — learning to be independent. In order to become less dependent, teens need to give new credence to their own ideas and opinions. They need additionally to believe that in separating from their parents they aren't losing so much. Separating from the people who love them the most would be overwhelming and cause incredible grief, if those people were not cut down to very human proportions.

"It can help to understand this process and give teens the freedom to have and voice their own opinions without verbally abusing parents and family. As the teen grows in competence and independence, of course, he or she will feel more secure and able to agree with you on occasion and to admire and accept you in new ways."

Behavior throughout adolescence is guided by the goal of wanting to belong and feeling significant. When children don't feel this way, they act in a way that seems like misbehavior. However, it is simply a misguided effort to find belonging and significance. This normal aspect of an adolescent's development becomes more problematic for teens who have lost touch with the creative, loving, powerful people they really are. Somewhere along the way they were taught that they were not good enough, not bright enough, not attractive enough, not energetic enough, not strong enough, etc. They took on these negative beliefs about themselves and used them as a foundation for their behavior. In other words, children act out because they have low self-esteem and, as a result, feel insecure. The following categories describe the ways a teenager (as well as younger children) might try to feel significant and how you, as a teacher, can manage their behavior.

DEMANDING UNDUE ATTENTION

The child's mistaken belief is that getting noticed equals being important in your eyes. He or she will try to keep you busy or get your attention for no reason. This desire for attention is often demonstrated when a student interrupts or becomes disruptive during a lesson. This is the "class clown" who is motivated by wanting to be noticed. Often, giving this child classroom responsibilities, such as erasing the blackboard, handing out papers or taking attendance, can be far more effective than punishing them for their outbursts.

REBELLION (REFUSAL TO PLAY BY THE RULES)

The need for adolescents to find out who they are by being independent often conflicts with the teacher's desire to retain decision-making authority. When not given input into the decision making process, teens may act out by associating with undesirable friends, doing poorly in academics, abusing drugs and alcohol or breaking rules and boundaries.

They want to give feedback and have choices rather than being given orders. Instead of focusing on and punishing them for rebellious behavior, try brainstorming and negotiation as a way of giving them a part in the decision making process. It's an art to do this while making it clear that certain rules still apply.

GETTING REVENGE

If a student is feeling insignificant or unloved, he or she may strike out by damaging property, being extremely disrespectful or doing something else to get even. Such actions are really a cry for help and an expression of inner hurt. Try not to take the child's behavior personally but, instead, help the child to communicate his or her feelings to you or a professional as a way of processing the hurt.

WITHDRAWAL

Although its outward appearance is very different from the other coping mechanisms, withdrawal, giving up and "caving in" are probably the most painful behavioral qualities for a child to endure. In essence, this child is asking to be respected and treated as worthwhile. Giving this child extra attention, warmth and acknowledgment is the approach that can heal this damaged ego.

We are involved in a more loving, empathetic approach when we focus on a child's insecurity and self-esteem issues and desire to feel significant as causes for misbehavior, rather than on the behavior itself. The following home assignment is intended to demonstrate this understanding at a deeper level.

159

THE EMPATHY EXERCISE

1. LIST THOSE THINGS THAT WERE IMPORTANT TO YOU AS A TEENAGER (E.G. CLOTHES, FRIENDS, PHYSICAL APPEARANCE, MUSIC, ETC.)

2. LIST THE VALUES AND SKILLS YOU WANT FOR YOUR STUDENTS BY THE TIME THEY ARE 21 (E.G. INDEPENDENCE, HONESTY, SELF-DISCIPLINE, ETC.)

160

3. IMAGINE THIS SCENARIO: A STUDENT REPEATEDLY WALKS IN LATE TO YOUR CLASS. WRITE DOWN HOW YOU WOULD REACT AND WHAT YOU WOULD SAY IN YOUR WORST MOMENTS.

4. GO OVER THE LIST OF VALUES AND SKILLS YOU WROTE DOWN IN QUESTION #2. IS YOUR REACTION TO THE SITUATION IN QUESTION #3 BRINGING YOUR STUDENTS CLOSER TO THESE VALUES AND SKILLS?

12

RESOLVING CONFLICT PEACEFULLY

Instead of me vs. you, we can reframe conflict as a way of working together to bring more wisdom and creativity into the problem solving process.

Today's youth get involved in more violent confrontations over less serious issues than at any other time in history. Violence permeates talk shows, music, movies, television and music videos at an extraordinary level. By the time the average American child is sixteen, he or she will view more than 200,000 acts of violence. The media portrays violence as glamorous and the preferred way of resolving conflict. As educators, we need to override this destructive influence by modeling ways of dealing with conflict situations in a peaceful, constructive and life supportive way.

HOW YOU RELATE TO THE ISSUE IS THE ISSUE

Before demonstrating peaceful resolution, we need to examine how we relate to the concept of conflict. Often people believe that opposition and the expression of feelings are counterproductive. Nothing could be further from the truth. **Conflict is a necessary, positive and an unavoidable part of any relationship.** Spirited disagreement and intellectual challenge can bind people into deeper and more meaningful relationships.

We must keep in mind that the classroom environment is greatly influenced by the way the teacher and students relate while processing issues. Often the first step in identifying and eventually resolving issues is to be in a setting that supports the honest expression of feelings. If discord is repressed and not resolved then resentments build up, feelings get displaced onto others and gossiping and backbiting are encouraged. James Baldwin summed it up when he said, **"Not everything that is faced can be changed but nothing can be changed until it is faced."**

SEVEN STEPS TO RESOLVING CONFLICT PEACEFULLY

1. **GET CLEAR ON YOUR INTENTION FOR A PEACEFUL RESOLUTION.** Instead of me vs. you, we can reframe conflict as a way of working together to bring more wisdom and intimacy into our relationships. This is quite different from the intention of hurting, attacking, putting down or proving that you are right.

In the Communication Chapter, I mentioned that before beginning a specific interaction that has the possibility of resulting in disharmony, we should ask ourselves, "Do I want peace or war?" The power of clarifying our intention is exemplified in this personal experience I often share with my high school students. After two years of research and observation, I finally completed the development of the program that I am currently presenting to students. I had a meeting with a headmaster who had expressed interest in incorporating my program into his school's curriculum. He was quite impressed and we set up a time and agreed to the salary I would be paid for teaching the program. Everything was set and I was to begin my first course in three weeks.

He was not available to talk when I called him a week later to work out a few small details. He didn't call back either. After unsuccessfully trying to reach him several times, I realized that he was not going to honor his agreement. Needless to say, I was very upset. About two months later I saw him walking toward me. I was really angry and my impulse was to verbally unload my hostility on him. As we approached each other I calmed down enough to ask myself, "What is my intention for this interaction? Do I want peace or war?" I chose peace. I began our conversation by telling him in an assertive way that I felt hurt and disappointed. He said that he felt bad but the school psychologist was threatened by my course and he had to make a choice. He apologized and gave me, along with his promise of a personal recommendation, the name of a headmaster who might be interested. After several meetings, his referral became the first school to present my program.

If my intention was war, I probably would have had an argument with the original headmaster and walked away with another enemy in my life. As a result of having the intention for peaceful resolution, I was given the opportunity to present my program for the first time. The power of intention is awesome. We create how our lives look at any particular moment by the choices we make. The clearer we are about our intention before we take action the more we will experience joy and fulfillment. Nike says, "Just Do It." I say, "Get clear on your intention, then Just Do It."

2. FORGIVE YOURSELF FOR ANY JUDGEMENTS YOU HAVE REGARDING YOUR BEHAVIOR WITH THE OTHER PERSON. This step was exemplified recently after an argument I had with one of my facilitators. I could have called him the next day in order to resolve the residual anger I felt. A week went by and, upon looking deeply, I saw that the reason I hadn't called was that I was ashamed of the anger I displayed during our disagreement. Once I forgave myself (and the judgments I had against myself for displaying anger), I was able to call him and begin the process of reconciliation.

163

Even if our intention is clear, we can delay the conversation that leads to resolution of a conflict because we have not forgiven the negative judgments we placed against ourselves

3. FEEL WHAT YOU ARE FEELING WITH NONJUDGMENTAL AWARENESS. This begins by feeling the specific physical sensations in our body. This process can be assisted by closing our eyes, which makes it easier to go inside.

Explorers of the human psyche, such as Gay Hendrix, Elizabeth Haye and Oschar Ichaso, among others, have investigated how specific emotions affect the functioning of different parts of the body. For instance, the jaws register anger, the throat and chest register loss and sadness, the stomach registers fear and the genitals register guilt. Focusing on the discomfort in our bodies assists us in identifying our present emotions as well as producing relevant images from our past that may be contributing to our present state. **Feelings are valuable in** that they tell us what is true for us in the moment. **Accessing them allows our intuition to guide us towards our next step.**

Instead of observing our bodies and emotions, we often go into our heads and try to figure things out. Thinking and rationalizing instead of feeling and sensing are ways of controlling our reality. It seems as if we spend a lot of our lives controlling, pretending and defending ourselves instead of being vulnerable and just feeling what we're feeling.

Even when we do feel, we have been taught which emotions are okay and which are not. Beliefs such as: "A decent person doesn't feel anger," "Feeling sexually attracted to someone is bad," "Men don't cry" and "Fear is bad" have greatly impaired our emotional expression. **Pain enters our lives every time there is a distance between how we really feel and how we think we are supposed to feel.** You get angry and instead of letting that feeling in, and feeling it for a few seconds, you rationalize, "I shouldn't be angry" or "It's really nothing." You see someone you're attracted to and instead of acting on that feeling you find a reason not to like them.

Feelings can never be denied or fixed, they just need to be acknowledged, experienced and observed. Instead of just experiencing feelings, we often turn to trying to control others, co-dependency and perfectionism. Food, alcohol and drug addictions are strategies also used in order not to feel what is going on inside ourselves. **A harmonious flow begins when we are able to sit with and accept, rather than intellectualize, suppress or deny what we are feeling.**

4. TAKE RESPONSIBILITY FOR YOUR FEELINGS AND YOUR PART IN THE CONFLICT. There is always the tendency to want to blame others. As we discussed in Chapter 7, Forgiveness, when we blame others we get to be right, justify our anger and not take responsibility for our part in the situation. We also get no true resolution. For there to be any possibility of resolving conflict peacefully, we must acknowledge our part in creating, promoting or allowing the conflict.

We next take responsibility for being the source of our anger. **Again,** nobody else makes us angry; we choose to get upset over someone else's behavior.

5. YOU NEXT NEED TO COMMUNICATE THE FUNDAMENTAL TRUTH OF WHAT YOU ARE FEELING. It can be short and honest with no blame intended. "I" statements are statements of truth and demonstrate a willingness to take responsibility rather than blame the other person. Some examples include:

"I feel treated unfairly"

"I feel disrespected"

"I feel hurt"

"I feel unloved"

Problems in relationship are more often caused by what we don't say rather than what we say. In order to relate openly, we have to be willing to be intimate with yourself and others. True intimacy begins by communicating our truth in the moment.

What often prevents us from communicating our inner truth can be traced back to childhood. At a point in our development we were made to feel that because of the behavior we were demonstrating, we were inadequate. Wanting to be loved, we developed a persona, an act that would guarantee that people would accept us. It becomes very difficult to communicate what is true for us in the moment when what we feel conflicts with this persona. For example, a three-year-old's parents didn't like it when she was disruptive and difficult. As a consequence, she learned to be a "good" girl so her parents would like her. After years. this persona has become so ingrained that she no longer sees it as an act but, instead, as who she really is.

Now she is 34, in a relationship, and when she gets angry, instead of communicating her anger, she has learned to be a "nice person" and nice people don't get angry. She is hindered in intimacy because she thinks that her boyfriend will not like her if she shows him the part that she hides.

Although we have adopted different characters, this scenario is

165

being played out in all our lives. Some of us have become the "angry person" who was made wrong as a child for showing his sensitivity; or the "aloof person" who was chastised for being too attached and needy; or the "clown" who couldn't get attention by being serious or real. Have you become the "intellectual" because you were rewarded with love for being so smart? Or are you the "rebel" who couldn't get enough attention by being good.

This next exercise will make us more aware of the habitual roles we play when conflict arises by defining our behavior in terms of what animal we most resemble

---

YOU'RE SUCH AN ANIMAL EXERCISE

A. Which animal most represents your style when conflict arises?

1. **SHEEP....**   "Whatever you say is fine"

   Advantage –   You are sensitive to others feelings and keep the peace in order to maintain relationships.

   Disadvantage –   Your needs are rarely met. You are left with anger and resentment.

2. **OSTRICH...**   "Leave me alone – I have nothing to do with it"

   Advantage –   You never get into a fight

   Disadvantage –   You feel powerless because you have no input into what goes on in your life.

3. **SHARK....**   "My way or the highway"

   Advantage –   You are always willing to speak up, take charge and take risks.

   Disadvantage –   You rarely really listen to others point of view. Winning is more important than relationships.

4. **OWL....**   "Let's work it out together"

   Advantage –   You respect others' point of view, and look for accommodation and compromise. You create trust and build relationships.

   Disadvantage –   It's not easy being an owl. It takes commitment and courage.

B. Why do you think you chose the role you chose? For example, "I became a sheep as a teenager because my parents gave me things when I didn't say anything and just went along with what they thought was right for me." Or, "I became a shark because my father was a shark and the only way he would listen is if I yelled louder than he did."

C. In another time in your life did your style resemble a different animal than it does now?

D. Which animal do you want to be like? What prevents you from being more like that animal?

In fact who we really are is none of these characters. Who we really are can't be defined because it is changing from moment to moment. It is our fixed persona that prevents us from responding genuinely to each moment.

---

6. **LISTEN SO YOU CAN ACKNOWLEDGE AND RESPECT THE OTHER PERSON'S PERSPECTIVE.** For there to be peaceful resolution we must be able to not only acknowledge that the other person has a point of view, but also to understand that their way of perceiving the situation is as valid to them as our interpretation is to us. In order to understand the other person's point of view, we must be able to listen. Once we do that, we can recognize the other person's needs, desires, priorities and values. As we discovered in the chapter on emotion coaching, the ability to empathize is a very important step in the process.

7. **LOOK FOR A SOLUTION WHERE BOTH PARTIES WIN.** This is difficult, but the intention for peace can evoke creative solutions to most problems. When adult and child utilize a consensus approach, no force is required in implementing the solution since the decision was mutually agreed upon. On the other hand, when the adult dictates and the child has no input in the decision-making process:

- The adult communicates that the child is not sensitive, resourceful or mature enough to find a solution.

- Children typically resist being told what to do.

- Since the child has no investment in the decision they have very little motivation to carry it out.

In the classroom, consensus based on choice can be very valuable. For example, giving a child a choice of books to read in order to bring a specific lesson forward gives the student a feeling of participation in her education process. Similarly, students input as to where they want to go on a field trip is another way of including them in the process.

First, identify the conflict, then generate and evaluate alternative solutions and finally find a solution that both parties can "live with". "Live with" does not mean "love" or "prefer", it means finding a solution that all involved are "willing to support".

169

NOBODY EVER SAID IT WAS EASY

Even if our intention for peaceful resolution is clear and we have promised ourselves that we will never yell again, the reality is that we sometimes let ourselves down. Just as in our approach to forgiveness, the acknowledgment and expression of anger is often a necessary step on the way to resolving conflict. In this chapter, the preferred path to peaceful resolution has been presented. It is an alternative and often very difficult approach for those of you who habitually attempt to resolve conflict by the verbal or physical expression of anger. It is not easy to change habit patterns. Again, acceptance and being gentle with ourselves especially at times when we think we have "blown it" is the most nurturing approach.

One other comment: Concise steps and numbered categories are often used in personal growth books and articles as a way of simplifying the process of dealing with life and its challenges. This approach seems to satisfy that lazy part of us that wants clear cut explanations without having to go through the effort of creative exploration. The steps presented in this chapter provide information and a framework for effectively dealing with emotional issues. They are not a magic bullet that, when employed correctly, will work in every conflict situation. When we have internalized the understanding, empathy and communication skills that are necessary for peaceful resolution, we will spontaneously know how to respond when conflict arises.

RESOLVING CONFLICT PEACEFULLY

There are seven principles that foster the peaceful resolution of a conflict situation:

1. HAVING THE INTENTION FOR PEACEFUL RESOLUTION
2. FORGIVE OURSELF FOR ANY JUDGEMENTS WE HAVE REGARDING OUR BEHAVIOR WITH THE OTHER PERSON
3. FEELING OUR FEELINGS
4. TAKING RESPONSIBILITY FOR OUR PART IN THE CONFLICT
5. COMMUNICATING OUR FEELINGS
6. HAVING EMPATHY FOR THE OTHER PERSON'S POINT OF VIEW
7. FINDING A SOLUTION WHERE BOTH PEOPLE WIN

171

1. REFLECT ON A RECENT ARGUMENT OR CURRENT DISAGREE-MENT YOU ARE HAVING WITH ANOTHER PERSON. DESCRIBE THE SPECIFICS OF THE CONFLICT AND WRITE ABOUT HOW YOU USED EACH OF THE ABOVE PRINCIPLES TO RESOLVE THIS CONFLICT.

_____

- In writing about her experience with a difficult student and the power of intention in resolving conflict, a teacher noted, "Besides being unruly, he usually was unprepared. I've publicly chided him in front of the class for his tardiness, lack of preparedness and poor academic production. That only seemed to make matters worse. I decided to change my approach.

  When I saw him in the hall during passing period I said, 'Good morning,' and told him that I hope to see him in class early — prepared to participate with the rest of his peers. Since doing this, his attitude and performance have changed. He needed to be disciplined in a sincere, loving manner in order for positive change to take place."

- After observing her passive communication pattern for a week, a teacher shared, "I noticed that I need to impress people or make people happy even at the expense of my own happiness. A lot of the things that I did this week had to do with me thinking that I had to make sure I did not put anyone in an uncomfortable situation, regardless of whether or not I was happy. I didn't want to bring people down, make people think less of me or disappoint anyone."

  This behavior is called worshipping the God of another's opinion.

- Another teacher shared, "My principal called me and somewhere in the conversation began to berate my colleague for an incident. He seemed to fault her for everything that was wrong with the world. Here's where I challenged my usual 'anything is better than conflict' approach. I decided that I would speak my mind. I let him know that I did not agree with him.

  The principal seemed to respect that I had the courage to question his opinion and that I felt at peace with myself."

13

IRRATIONAL BELIEFS
AND DESTRUCTIVE HABITS

Becoming a masterful teacher requires identifying and changing the irrational beliefs that influence our perceptions of ourselves, others and the world.

When we were very young, we viewed reality in innocence. Each moment was fresh and new because we had very few beliefs about the world to color what we saw. As adults, however, we have acquired all sorts of beliefs about others, the world and ourselves. Whether these beliefs are hidden or not, they cloud our perception and as a result influence our behavior.

On close examination, we find that many of these beliefs are contradictory, based on single instances that we have unwisely turned into generalizations. The psychologist Albert Ellis has called these "irrational beliefs." For example, some of us carry in our minds the idea that overweight people are lazy, unhealthy and sad. However, we also think of this group as "jolly." Clearly, both of these generalizations cannot be true. In fact, neither of them is. Until we examine such hidden irrational beliefs, they remain uncontested and continue to influence our perceptions and actions.

Irrational beliefs are the basis for all stereotypes. When we assume an attitude toward someone we are meeting for the first time, we are responding to a stereotype we carry within us. "You are Jewish, therefore..." "You are black, therefore..." "You are a woman, therefore..." "You are rich... poor... old... fat...." You name it, if there's a stereotype then there's also an irrational belief to match.

Rational beliefs, on the other hand, are beliefs based on unwavering facts. They can be proven true in every case. I believe, for example, that if I let go of my pen, it will drop to the floor. I can test this and prove it by getting the same result every time. Irrational beliefs, however, do not stand up to the test of what is true in reality.

As we've discussed throughout this book, many of our beliefs come from the past. If a dog once bit me, I may see all dogs, even the gentlest of pups, as vicious and dangerous. Some irrational beliefs are simply prejudices we have acquired from our parents or the communities in which we were raised. Beliefs like, "All rich people get their money by lying and cheating" or "Poor people are too lazy to work and make money" or "Crying is a sign of weakness" are irrational because they cannot be consistently shown to be true.

IRRATIONAL BELIEFS ABOUT OURSELVES

Irrational beliefs not only influence the way we view others but they distort the way we see ourselves. Let's discuss a few of these irrational beliefs about ourselves:

I LOSE MY POWER IF I ALLOW MYSELF TO BE VULNERABLE.

Many of us struggle or have struggled with this one. The reason is plain to see: all of us, at one time or another, have been hurt by someone who took advantage of our vulnerability. On some level, we were all betrayed by parents who could never match the love we had for them when we were young. Maybe it was another family member, partner, or friend whom we felt betrayed us. Nevertheless, it is irrational to believe that being vulnerable always results in pain and loss of power. **Allowing ourselves to be vulnerable, especially in intimate relationships, is necessary to establish the trust that makes love possible.**

Adopting the above irrational beliefs is a way of eliminating from our lives the pain caused by relationships. Similarly, irrational beliefs such as: "Men can't be trusted," "I have lost the only person I could ever love," "Men are incapable of making commitments," and "Relationships are just about suffering, so why bother?" are also often manifestations of fear. These beliefs may serve the function of protecting us from the reoccurrence of past hurts but the price we pay is often decreased vitality, isolation and a lost opportunity to experience the joy and lessons learned from being intimate with another person.

I SHOULD FEEL BAD FOR A LONG TIME AFTER I DO SOMETHING WRONG.

This is an irrational belief that causes many of us a great deal of unnecessary suffering. This particular belief is rooted in the superstition: "If I make myself feel bad enough for long enough, then the heavens or God or fate will have mercy on me and not punish me too badly." This belief usually comes from childhood experience when "the heavens" meant our parents or other adults in authority. Perhaps they even abused that authority by supporting this belief. In any case, what possible good can come from feeling bad for a long time? Guilt only produces resentment towards ourselves and others. Looking at mistakes as an opportunity to learn rather than as a time to beat ourselves up seems to be a more rational approach.

175

Almost any belief about ourselves that begins with "I should..." is irrational. We need to meet and accept ourselves where we are. Otherwise we hurt ourselves by applying stereotypes to ourselves. Here are just a few of the many irrational beliefs we have about ourselves that cause confusion and suffering:

- Because I have failed at _____, I am a worthless person.
- Other people cause me to be angry.
- A man should deal with his problems on his own.
- Being able to take pain makes me more manly.
- When people act unfairly, I should blame them and see them as wicked individuals.
- Emotional misery comes from outside of me.
- The influence of the past cannot be eradicated.

- Women should never show anger.

- If something seems fearsome, I have no choice but to preoccupy myself with worrying about it.

- Life would be easy if I had money.

- If I don't fight back, I'm a wimp.

- I should be nice to everyone.

- I should be thinner.

IRRATIONAL BELIEFS ABOUT OTHER PEOPLE

Irrational beliefs about others not only hurt them, but also ourselves because we are weakened whenever we disengage and take our hearts away. The "shoulds" we inflict on others also keep us from seeing what other people have to offer. Here are a couple of examples:

OLD PEOPLE ARE WISE.
This is a stereotype. This particular irrational belief, common in our culture, may seem positive on the surface. (Certainly it's better than "old people are stupid.") However, it still takes the irrational step of identifying people's status (wise) with a category (old people.) In working with both parents and children, I have found many youngsters who were much wiser than their parents. If people became wiser as they grew older then the world, by now, would be a peaceful and prosperous paradise, wouldn't it?

Irrational beliefs that create expectations can place unreasonable demands on people. The idea that all blacks are good athletes, all Chinese are mathematical geniuses or all Italians are great cooks often places a great deal of pressure on members of these groups. All of these beliefs have power over us when they are hidden but don't hold up when we stop and examine them.

KIDS TODAY ARE ROTTEN.

This belief comes from newspapers, TV and films. Sadly, we find few positive and well-rounded portraits of teens in the media. Remember that there is a simple scientific test for a rational belief (like letting go of the pen and watching it drop to the floor) — it must be able to be tested and proven true in every case. Clearly, using this guideline, the statement that, "kids today are rotten," is an irrational belief. Besides, if you stop to think about it, adults have always been saying this about "kids today". This next quote exemplifies just how long adults have been complaining about kids.

"The children now love luxury; they have bad manners; contempt for authority; show disrespect for elders...Children are now tyrants, not the servants of their households...They contradict their parents...and tyrannize their teachers."

Socrates, c. 390 B.C.

It's easy to acquire a head full of irrational beliefs about other people. Prejudices and stereotypes are always readily available. Here are some other irrational beliefs about other people. How many of them do you recognize as, at least sometimes, your own?

- People should turn out better then they do.
- Women should be married by 30.
- This is the way teenagers are and they'll probably never change.
- A teenager doesn't really know what's best for him/her.
- People who work with their hands are not as smart as people who work in offices.
- People who smoke are too weak to quit.
- People who go to church are good; people who don't are bad.
- New Yorkers are cold and unfriendly.

- Lawyers are crooks.

- White southerners are racists.

- Men are insensitive.

- People who are overweight don't have will power.

- Rich people are arrogant.

IRRATIONAL BELIEFS ABOUT RELATIONSHIPS

Along with our irrational beliefs about ourselves and others, most of us find that we have quite a few irrational beliefs about relationships as well. For example:

IF YOU LOVE SOMEONE, THEN YOU DON'T FIGHT AND ARGUE WITH HIM OR HER.

It is my experience that the exact opposite belief is more often true: The people we love are the people we tend to argue with the most. As stated previously, the ones we love hurt us the most deeply and as a result, trigger emotional reactions. Intimate relationships provide us with the opportunity to heal that part of ourselves that was damaged at an earlier stage of development. Part of this healing process is the triggering of past emotions that were never completely resolved. According to Harville Hendrix, the function of love is to bring up and heal everything that is not love. By viewing this as one of the main functions of a relationship, we make room for the discord that occurs in every intimate relationship.

Think about it: arguing and trying to persuade someone else of your point of view are ways of saying, "I care about what you think." If this were not true, you would simply walk away, wouldn't you? The truth is that successful couples find ways to disagree that do not violate each other's dignity and do not damage the relationship.

A PERSON WHO REALLY LOVED ME WOULD KNOW HOW I FEEL AND WHAT I NEED WITHOUT MY HAVING TO TELL THEM.
This particular irrational belief may be the single biggest producer of pain and sadness in relationships. It is a combination of fairy tale romance and a superstitious view of love as something that is "true" or not, instead of something two people create and nurture together. Even the most compatible people cannot always know what each other is thinking. Empathy is not mind reading. This irrational belief is a totally useless excuse for poor communication. Let me offer you a rational belief to replace it: **Relationships are nurtured when people clearly communicate their needs, feelings, and desires.**

Irrational beliefs about relationships are especially painful because they are based on blame. Nobody comes out unhurt when these beliefs are operating. Let's look at a few others. Recognize any of them?

- If you hurt me, I have no choice but to hurt you back.

179

- It is bad to be jealous.

- People have to earn my forgiveness.

- If I close my heart, it will hurt the other person and I will win.

- When a relationship ends, the person who leaves first is the winner.

- When a relationship starts to feel routine, it's over.

- When I do something nice for someone, they should return the favor.

- I will never make it longer than a year in a relationship.

- Relationships are made in heaven.

- If this relationship doesn't work out, I'll never find anyone else.

- If I ever left him, he couldn't go on without me.

- You should always feel passion toward the one you love.

IRRATIONAL BELIEFS ABOUT PARENTS AND CHILDREN

Since many teachers are parents, have parents and often deal with their students' parents, let's look at some commonly held, often hidden irrational beliefs about parents and children. You will find a lot of "shoulds" in here — a tip-off that we have left the world of rational expectations behind and entered the "Twilight Zone" of irrational beliefs.

I AM NOT A GOOD PARENT UNLESS I GIVE MY CHILDREN EVERYTHING THEY WANT.

Hardly any of us would actually agree with this statement but remember that most irrational beliefs are hidden; they operate below the level of awareness. This is one of the harder ones to change because we are swimming against the tide of our consumer culture which sends us this message every day through TV, radio, magazines, and movies. Our kids get their daily dose of this toxic message too and this can make it especially difficult. It is, after all, the job of advertisers to get kids to want things and to get you to feel guilty enough to pay for those things. If we examine this irrational belief, we see that, of course, giving our children whatever they want does not make us good parents.

Sadly, I have known several children from extremely wealthy households who got everything they ever asked for. However, they didn't get the things that count for a great deal more: guidance, support, examples of good judgment and a sense of balance in their lives.

On the other side, I have had economically less fortunate parents say, "I resented my parents for giving me very little materially when I was growing up and I am trying to give my child everything they want." These are the same parents who often speak about not having enough money to buy necessities for themselves. Kids are very smart and can be extremely manipulative. I have seen them become extremely spoiled and demanding using this attitude to their advantage. It is my observation that giving based on past disappointment and guilt does not serve us or our children.

IF I DO AND SAY ALL THE RIGHT THINGS, MY CHILDREN WILL COMMUNICATE WITH ME OPENLY AND HONESTLY.

This is another irrational belief not worth the suffering it causes. It is a reflection of the equally irrational belief that our children are merely reflections of ourselves. Children are people, not products. When we model good communication for our children, we do it because it is right, because we love them and because they need that demonstration. We cannot expect them to always follow our lead. We need to respect the fact that our children have their own process and it is important to allow them to be vague or remain silent when they feel it is appropriate.

PARENTS SHOULD NEVER APOLOGIZE TO THEIR CHILDREN.

This irrational belief stems from the feeling that parents must always maintain the upper hand. Perhaps this belief came from our families or our culture but like all other irrational beliefs, it falls flat in the face of reason. This is real life, not an imaginary world where parents are always kind, gentle, understanding, patient and right. We are people. We make mistakes. That's why pencils have erasers and people have apologies. We need to develop the humility and honesty that make us able to apologize to children when we have behaved in a manner that does not serve them. This vulnerability creates intimacy and trust and demonstrates a deep level of integrity.

Although we have acquired many irrational beliefs, it seems as if adults become even more susceptible to their influence when they become parents. Parents want so much to do the right thing. There's nothing wrong with high standards, but as we have seen, irrational beliefs are something different, they do nothing to improve our lives or the lives of children. They undermine us, frustrate our intentions and rob us of the joy that can be ours. Here are a number of other irrational beliefs I have discovered while working with parents:

I JUDGE MY SUCCESS AS A PARENT BY HOW WELL MY CHILD LOOKS, DRESSES, SOCAILIZES AND WHAT THEY ACHIEVE.

"Producing" a child who is "extremely bright", "gifted", "polite" and/or "a great athlete" has become a status symbol for many parents. Often, these parents are unfulfilled in their own lives, and use their children as a source of self-worth and self-esteem. In many cases, they look to their child for the satisfaction and pleasure lacking in their relationship with their spouse, or as a substitute for intimate adult relationships. These circumstances often produce an overprotective, critical environment where the child is unduly pressured academically and socially.

In many cases, "producing" a "special" son or daughter is more attractive and less difficult than maintaining an intimate, loving adult relationship. A spouse often runs a distant second to the child for attention and nurturing. However, nothing has a greater impact on the social and emotional well-being of a child than the quality of relationship of the adults they observe day in and day out-their parents.

There are a number of single parents participating in our programs that have not healed their own wounds. They are motivated to "produce" overly independent children who will avoid the pain of being dependent on another person (spouse) for fulfillment. There is nothing wrong with having children develop into independent, free-thinking adults; but the outcomes are quite different when the message is driven by unresolved anger, non-forgiveness and hurt rather than what is best for the child.

Other irrational beliefs parents harbor are:

- Parents should be perfect.
- It's my job to keep my child from experiencing pain and failure.
- Parents are the only key to a child's success.
- My child lives in my house, I pay for everything, so he must listen, do his chores and spend his money exactly how I want him to.
- I know what my children really need, so I'm the best one to plan activities for them
- Good parents never lose patience with their children.
- Good parents never hit their children.

EDUCATION FOR TRANSFORMATION

- A parent always knows what is best for their children.
- A teenager doesn't really know what's best for him/her.
- (For single parents): My child would do much better if his father/mother was around.
- I shouldn't have been so lenient when he was little.
- I know best with who my child should be friends with.
- I am a failure because I got divorced.

IRRATIONAL BELIEFS ABOUT TEACHING

Just as doctors "should" always be totally compassionate; lawyers "should" only protect the innocent; politicians "should" always be honest; policemen "should" always be tolerant; the profession of teaching also has its share of "shoulds".

OBEDIENCE IS MORE IMPORTANT THAN HAVING A CHILD WHO THINKS, IS RESPONSIBLE, EXPRESSIVE AND WHO LEARNS FROM HIS OR HER MISTAKES.

It's unfortunate that often a great deal of classroom time is spent keeping one or two unruly students in line. But what about the child who quietly sits in class, never speaks out of turn, does every homework assignment well and never causes a disruption — the student who doesn't participate but gets good grades. Often these students feel insecure and aren't doing too well in the area of relationship. Are we really serving these students by not encouraging them to take risks and to be more assertive and communicative? Because of their inner discipline, ability to pay attention and the value they place on education, many of these students may become our future leaders. This will not become a reality unless we help them to express who they are and what they need in every moment. These two important factors will help develop the self-esteem necessary for them to effectively interact with others.

I AM NOT A GOOD TEACHER IF STUDENTS DON'T DO WELL IN MY CLASS.

We have a professional obligation to do everything possible to help a failing student function more satisfactorily. Interventions such as altering lesson plans to better meet the needs of a specific student, trying new teaching techniques, working with a student's parents and spending extra time after class with the student are all ways of helping. But we must also realize that there may be variables beyond our control that affect a student's academic performance. Certain students, for one reason or another, are just not ready to do well in a particular subject.

BECAUSE I AM A TEACHER I MOST LIKELY WILL NOT EARN MUCH MONEY

This is similar to the starving artist syndrome. I am an educator and I am making more money than most teachers. I also know that I am going to become very comfortable financially as a result of teaching, writing, lecturing and developing courses for public education. These options as well as others are open to all educators but many teachers limit their financial potential because they believe that being in education means not making a great deal of money.

I CAN'T GET RICH DOING SOMETHING I LOVE.

On the contrary... We deserve to be financially secure through if we love what we are doing and we are good at it. Again, the starving artist perception can work against us.

A GOOD TEACHER DOESN'T GET EMOTIONALLY UPSET WITH THEIR STUDENTS.

Just because we don't always behave the way we think we "should" in front of our class, it does not mean that we are bad teachers. Does a parent have to always be emotionally balanced when dealing with their children to be "good"? If that were the case, there would not be any "good" parents.

IRRATIONAL BELIEFS EXERCISE

1. WRITE DOWN YOUR NEXT BIG GOAL.

2. WRITE DOWN A LIST OF ALL THE POSITIVE BELIEFS AND A LIST OF ALL THE NEGATIVE BELIEFS ASSOCIATED WITH THE ACCOMPLISHMENT OF YOUR GOAL.

   POSITIVE BELIEFS

   NEGATIVE BELIEFS

3. ARE THERE ANY IRRATIONAL BELIEFS OPERATING THAT COULD BE AFFECTING THE ACCOMPLISHMENT OF YOUR GOAL?

185

DESTRUCTIVE HABITS

Like irrational beliefs, many habits have been passed down to us by others. For instance, we learned how to communicate by observing our parents. The manner in which we organize our homes has been greatly influenced by the environment we were brought up in. Or, we may have become teenage smokers as a result of observing older people smoke. Interestingly, there are also instances where people have cultivated traits that are the opposite of what they observed or were taught at an early age. For example, there are people who have developed a very aggressive mode of expression because they do not want to be like their passive fathers or mothers.

Remember the exercise in the Acceptance home assignment that dealt with accepting our every thought, feeling and action in each moment? There are certain destructive habits that we have developed as a way of coping with thoughts, feelings and actions that we are unable to accept and unwilling to experience. Habitually having a "social" drink because of not wanting to accept the uncomfortable feeling of meeting a new person, eating sweets instead of accepting a feeling of sadness or overworking as a way of avoiding what is going on in our life emotionally are all ways of avoiding our feelings.

AWARENESS COUNTS

For change to occur we must first have awareness. For example, we became better listeners when we became aware of what we did instead of listening. We communicated more effectively when we became aware of the habitual patterns of communication that were not serving us.

Likewise, an important step in transforming habits that do not serve us is to take them from the domain of habits into the light of awareness. We do this by asking ourselves, in each moment, why we are doing what we are doing. For example, instead of habitually lighting a cigarette ask yourself: "Why am I lighting this cigarette?" "What feelings am I having that I'm unwilling to accept or experience?" This challenge can be used for any habit... "Why am I eating now when I'm not even hungry?" "Why am I sitting here staring at the TV when I have so much work to do?" "Why am I talking about this person behind his back?"

Questioning behavior that does not serve us brings it into conscious awareness and is a key step in the process towards change.

ANOTHER MENTION OF INTENTION

Once again, the importance of the power of intention comes into play. It is obvious that change does not occur until we first have the intention to change. For most people it seems natural to follow the intention to change with an effort to eliminate the specific habit. This is a great idea except that it usually doesn't work. How many times have you failed at eliminating smoking, overeating, rushing, uncontrollable anger, lateness, etc.?

Our chances for success are significantly increased when we ask ourselves: "What is my intention regarding this area of my life?" For instance: "I want to be more vital and have more socializing in my life" is a different starting point than "I want to lose weight." "I want to be able to breathe easily, feel healthier and not always be coughing" is different from "I want to stop smoking." The intention of wanting a more loving and peaceful relationship with your wife has more power than "I want to stop yelling and screaming."

Up to now, many of you have been trying the elimination approach. I am asking you to try focusing on a positive intention for a specific area of your life and see if that doesn't work better for you.

One final observation about the nature of intention and our power as creators: **The universe supports us when we get clear on what we want. If it's for our highest good, it will be given to us just because we have asked for it.**

DO YOU DESERVE WHAT YOU ARE ASKING FOR?

You may be jumping up and down with the realization that the game is final ly over now that you have understood that all there is to do for change to occur is to be aware of a specific habit and have the intention for positiv change. I hate to burst your bubble but we've only just begun.

Earlier we mentioned that "nobody is going to give you what you don think you deserve." **The intentions we have for ourselves reflect what w think we deserve.** We can apply this concept by looking at and possibl upgrading our intention for specific areas of our lives. Are you living at th material level you would like? What do you feel you deserve regarding mate rial well being? What beliefs have prevented you from setting your inten tions higher? Are you willing to upgrade your intention?

Regarding your health and physical appearance: Are you functioning a optimum health? Do you feel comfortable at your present weight? Are yo willing to upgrade your intention regarding your physical appearance?

Regarding your primary relationship: What is your intention for futur growth and expansion? Are you willing to upgrade your intentions? If yo are not presently involved in a relationship, what qualities do you think yo deserve in your next one?

We can have awareness and intention, but the life transformation tha occurs through changing destructive habits may not occur until we are will ing to look at the source of our beliefs concerning our capacity and our righ to manifest our full potential at every level. There are several deep-seate irrational beliefs that we may have acquired somewhere along the way tha can be subtly influencing our ability to manifest our desires:

- I AM NOT WORTHY OF SUCCESS
- GOD IS AGAINST ME
- IF I HAVE THIS MUCH FEAR INSIDE OF ME THEN I DON'T DESERVE ANY TYPE OF REWARD

Before I started observing them, these irrational beliefs were operating at an unconscious and very subtle way to undermine fulfillment and positive change in my life. For example, I would get angry when there was a light ning storm and my phone would not work. Being aware that we get angry because life doesn't show up the way we think it "should" is one level of understanding. At a deeper level, I began to see that underneath my anger was the belief that God was making my life difficult because he didn't like me. More often than not, recalling this understanding when the opportunity for upset occurs, dissipates the anger and produces a calmer response.

Again, there are times when I am not proud of my emotional response to a situation. After an outburst I sometimes think, "How can I teach social and emotional skills if I can't control my own emotions?" This is irrational and destructive. If we had to wait until we were perfect to teach anything, nothing would ever get taught.

Another area where the issue of worthiness comes into play is when we have to decide whether we deserve to buy something for ourselves. Have you ever seen an item of clothing that you liked and could afford to buy but don't? What was keeping you from making that purchase? Very often it's the feeling that you don't deserve it. I equate self-worth with self-nurturing. This refers to Chapter 3 where we spoke about the importance of taking care of ourselves physically, emotionally, mentally and spiritually.

Throughout this book I have been asking you to consider choices that will nurture you in every area of your life. Forgiving ourselves and others, taking responsibility for creating what occurs in our lives, accepting ourselves and others and speaking our truth in a considerate manner are all ways of nurturing ourselves. The question is: **"Do we love ourselves enough to do what is best for ourselves in every moment?"**

Once we become aware of a habit that we may never have thought about before (for example, learning that it doesn't serve us to indulge the negative voice inside of ourselves) we then have the choice to change. What is it that could allow this habit to continue even though we now know that it doesn't serve us and that a better choice is available? First of all, it is the nature of a habit to continually repeat itself. We can't stop our negative self-talk from appearing; but what we can do, once it

189

begins, is not feed it. How long are you willing to allow this negative talk to continue inside of you? Is it five seconds, five minutes, five hours, or five days? This is where choice and will (or won't) power come into play. It is my experience that how long I am willing to let negativity continue once it has begun has to do with how willing I am to nurture myself and not let it continue. This applies not only to negative self-talk but to habits such as negatively judging others, overeating, impatience, procrastination, etc. Think about it. At every moment are you your own best friend? **At every moment are you doing whatever it takes to nurture yourself?** If not...then why not?

Maybe our parents, society, a teacher, a sibling, a peer or all of them told us we were not good enough. After many generations, maybe we were born with a feeling of lack. I am not exactly sure how negative beliefs about our self-worth became so deeply imbedded in our consciousness but I do know that they are there and that these beliefs don't serve us in becoming fulfilled human beings. Let me reinforce this point by once again quoting Nelson Mandela's 1994 Inaugural Address:

> "Our worst fear is not that we are inadequate. Our deepest fear is that we are powerful beyond measure. It is our light not our darkness that most frightens us. We ask ourselves who am I to be brilliant, gorgeous, talented and fabulous. Actually, who are you not to be? You are a child of God. Your playing small doesn't serve the world. There is nothing enlightened about shrinking so that others don't feel insecure around you. We were born to make manifest the glory of God within us. It is in everyone and as we let our own light shine we unconsciously give other people permission to do the same. As we are liberated from our fear our presence automatically liberates others."

DESTRUCTIVE HABITS

FROM THE LIST ON THE NEXT PAGE, PICK ONE DESTRUCTIVE HABIT YOU WOULD LIKE TO CHANGE. THEN ASK YOURSELF:

1. WHY DO I DO IT AND HOW DOES IT AFFECT ME?

2. WHAT IS MY POSITIVE INTENTION FOR THIS PART OF YOUR LIFE?

3. WHAT DO I DESERVE?

4. WHAT CAN I DO DIFFERENTLY?

5. WHAT HAPPENS WHEN I DO IT DIFFERENTLY?

Remember, we have been practicing some of these destructive habits for years, perhaps for most of our lives. Again, be patient and loving toward yourself. Personal transformation isn't easy nor does it happen overnight.

LIST OF DESTRUCTIVE HABITS

1. Putting things off (procrastinating)
2. Working too hard - or not working hard enough
3. Ignoring problems
4. Arguing
5. Over-sleeping or not getting enough sleep
6. Abusing sugar
7. Talking about others behind their backs
8. Making excuses
9. Starting things and not finishing them
10. Not saying what you really want to say.
11. Overeating or not eating enough
12. Being disorganized or being too organized
13. Not telling the truth
14. Worrying
15. Abusing drugs or alcohol
16. Gossiping
17. Making fun of others
18. Saying "yes" when you want to say "No"
19. Being late
20. Always rushing
21. Not listening
22. Blaming others
23. Interrupting others when they're talking
24. Watching TV
25. Not setting priorities
26. Letting your jealousy, envy, anger or other emotions run you
27. Wasting time
28. Giving advice that isn't asked for
29. Spending more money than you earn
30. Talking too much
31. Being a chronic complainer

32. Forgetting names or other important things
33. Being overcritical of others
34. Not taking care of details
35. Smoking
36. Losing things

PARTICIPANTS' COMMENTS

- A teacher commented, "In my former school, about three quarters of the way through the school year, a new student was placed in my class. I immediately came to the conclusion that the young lady was going to be a problem because troublemakers transfer to schools in the middle of a semester. The young lady was over six feet tall and weighed over 200 pounds. I immediately thought this young lady was a bully, and as a result of this prejudgment, I did not care for her. Although I had not received her records nor spoken to anyone about her, I had formulated my own conclusions. As a result, I never made her feel welcome. I realize now that this affected her performance in the class."

- A woman confided that she felt like a failure and was very unsure of herself regarding her parenting skills because her 22-year-old son was serving time in jail for attempted robbery. One of the things we discussed was her Irrational Beliefs such as:

  If I'd been a good parent, my child would never have gone to jail.
  It's my job as a parent to keep my child from experiencing pain.
  My value as a human being is determined by how my child turns out.

  Along with these observations the class had incredible empathy for her process.

- A father shared that no matter what he did, his 16-year-old son would not talk to him. He mentioned how his neighbor and his neighbor's son always talked and had a good time together. He said he was even trying to tape messages for his son. He had tried almost everything in an effort to communicate. I pointed out several Irrational Beliefs that he was demonstrating:

  If my kid doesn't talk to me, it's because I've failed as a parent.
  I pay for my son's clothes, rent, transportation, food, etc. The least he could do is talk to me.

Our discussion brought up the following questions: "Did you ever just accept how your son was regarding his communication with you?" "Did you ever consider that your son's desire not to communicate with you might have nothing to do with you?" "Maybe you shouldn't take his behavior personally." He said he'd never considered these possibilities. Like a lot of males, he was very action oriented, and just wanted to fix the problem. I also pointed out that teenagers have a tough process. They are at an age when there is a pressing need to separate from their parents in order to establish their own identities. Yet they rely on their parents for food, shelter and clothing. Not communicating is a way to have some control in an environment where they have very little control.

- A drug counselor shared that he felt like a failure each time one of his patients went back to drugs. This was again an example of the irrational belief: "If my patient fails, it's my fault." We can do the best we can to be of service but in the end people are responsible for their own evolution.

- A teacher in my course spoke about how upset she would get when she couldn't "reach" a student. Again, the Irrational Belief: "It's my fault if a student doesn't respond."

   My position as a teacher is that I try as hard as I can to reach each student. The reality is that not every student is ready to hear what I have to teach. Not only is this my experience as a teacher. As a student, I have not always been ready to hear what was being presented.

- A male teacher once told me, "When I go to the movies and I see a man cry, it really makes me sick. I want to throw up. When my father died," he went on, "my three brothers and I were standing around the casket checking each other out to make sure none of us cried."

   This man was a wonderful teacher who was only beginning to

see that some of his beliefs were irrational and a product of cultural cross-wiring.

- A teacher said that she wanted to figure out how she could live more efficiently so she wouldn't be rushing so much. What I noticed while she was speaking about her pattern of rushing was that she didn't seem to enjoy what she was doing while she was doing it. It seemed that her enjoyment came from placing completion checks on her "to do" list.

  Gradually, it became evident that her lesson was more about enjoying what she was doing as she was doing it rather than doing less. Dislodging the Irrational Beliefs that fueled her habit of rushing, that she would be happier if she were able to check more things off on her list, was the key that opened the door to change.

- A parent, who had too much to do and not enough time in the day to finish her tasks, dealt with her destructive habit of not getting enough sleep by allocating more responsibilities to her children. "Instead of checking their homework I trusted that they were doing a good job. I had them wash their own clothes and do the dishes instead of my doing it. I paid them for doing these chores so it became a win-win situation."

- A teacher, while focusing on her destructive habit of doing things at the last minute, realized that although this habit produced stress she actually enjoyed, and functioned very effectively, under pressure. She realized that her habit of waiting until the last minute actually served her.

- After working on the destructive habit of saying "yes" when she wanted to say "no," a teacher responded: "Sometimes I feel I may hurt someone's feelings if I say 'no.' When I say 'yes' when I really want to say 'no,' I could kick myself. I get angry at myself and at the person I said 'yes' to. Of course, I never tell them or let them know I am angry. Sometimes I feel used, even though I know it was my choice to say 'yes'. After reading the assignment, I decided that if the situation arose again, I would say what I really wanted to say. There were two times last week when something was asked of me where I felt it was expected that I say 'yes'. I told both people, 'no'. The result was that I felt better about my choices. I didn't have any turmoil within me about what I should or should not have said. I didn't feel as if I was doing something that I didn't want to do, either."

198

14

CULTURAL DIVERSITY

What is more destructive than being prejudiced is not realizing when we are being prejudiced.

I am far from an expert when it comes to understanding the specific traits of people from various cultures. What interests me more than the differences are the prejudices and irrational beliefs that individuals hold towards other groups of people. Prejudice in itself is negative — when we prejudge anyone, we are doing them and ourselves a disservice. But what is far more destructive is being prejudiced and not realizing our prejudiced. It's like any other negative, unconscious pattern of behavior: until we become aware of it, there is nothing we can do to change it. This brief chapter will focus on exercises that are intended to make us more aware of our prejudices and the stereotypes that prejudice is based upon. We are all prejudiced towards some group at some level. I am asking you to honestly look at prejudices that you may never have been aware of before.

For those of you that don't think you are prejudiced and never prejudge anyone, please take a look at this list:

Old people
Adolescents
Jehovah's witnesses
Rich people
"Old money"
"New money"
Smokers
Hassidic Jews
Fat people

Black men with gold in their teeth
Black men with white women
White men with black women
Kids with pierced tongues
People with tattoos
Men
Lesbians and gays
People who are prejudiced
Pakistanis
Southerners
Arabs
Puerto Ricans
Dominicans
African Americans
People with AIDS
Asians

People who ask for money on the street
Churchgoers
West Indians
Africans
Women
Kids who wear baggy pants down around their knees
People who are bald

Do you still feel exempt? Try these next two exercises to see where you might be prejudging others.

For this exercise rate each group from 1 to 5 for each statement:

1=Always true (90% or more of the time)
2=Often true (75% of the time)
3=Sometimes true (50% of the time)
4=Rarely true (25% of the time)
5=Never true (less than 10% of the time)

	PRN	WHT	BLK	JEW	MEX	RCH
1. Tend to be poor	—	—	—	—	—	—
2. Are similar in behavior to other groups	—	—	—	—	—	—
3. Have superior athletic ability	—	—	—	—	—	—
4. Will seek to exploit others	—	—	—	—	—	—
5. Tend to keep to themselves and are suspicious of others	—	—	—	—	—	—
6. Are generally tolerant of other people	—	—	—	—	—	—
7. Lack initiative are lazy and are not dependable	—	—	—	—	—	—
8. Are extremely ambitious, capable and intelligent	—	—	—	—	—	—
9. Discriminate against others	—	—	—	—	—	—
10. Become wealthy by manipulation and cheating	—	—	—	—	—	—
11. Will always remain a foreign and alien element	—	—	—	—	—	—
12. Are mostly patriotic	—	—	—	—	—	—
13. Will more then likely succeed in education	—	—	—	—	—	—
14. Fail to keep up their personal appearance and their neighborhood	—	—	—	—	—	—
15. Practice strange customs	—	—	—	—	—	—
16. Are cunning and proud	—	—	—	—	—	—

	PRN	WHT	BLK	JEW	MEX	RCH	ASIA
17. Are often too emotional	___	___	___	___	___	___	___
18. Discriminate against others	___	___	___	___	___	___	___
19. Prove to be as trustworthy as others	___	___	___	___	___	___	___
20. Control most of our economic institutions	___	___	___	___	___	___	___

*KEY

PR=Puerto Ricans   WHT=Whites   BLK=Blacks

JEW=Jewish People   MX=Mexicans   RCH=Rich People

ASIA=Asian People

r this exercise rate each group from 1 to 5 for each statement:

	PRN	WHT	BLK	JEW	MEX	RCH	ASIA
	—	—	—	—	—	—	—
IND 1.......5 CRUEL							
	—	—	—	—	—	—	—
ONEST 1........5 DISHONEST							
	—	—	—	—	—	—	—
APPY 1........5 SAD							
	—	—	—	—	—	—	—
UIET 1........5 LOUD							
	—	—	—	—	—	—	—
ARDWORKING 1.......5 LAZY							
	—	—	—	—	—	—	—
RAVE 1........5 COWARDLY							
	—	—	—	—	—	—	—
ICH 1........5 POOR							
	—	—	—	—	—	—	—
NTELLIGENT 1.......5 IGNORANT							
	—	—	—	—	—	—	—
EACEFUL 1.......5 WARLIKE							

Research has shown that an important factor in developing self-esteem is being proud of one's own culture. Here is an exercise that is fun to do in a culturally diverse group, but also has value when done alone.

1. WHAT IS YOUR CULTURAL BACKGROUND?

2. WHAT DO YOU REALLY LIKE ABOUT YOUR CULTURE?

3. WHAT CULTURAL TRADITIONS HAVE BEEN PASSED DOWN TO YOU FROM YOUR FAMILY?

204

4. WHAT STORIES HAVE BEEN PASSED ON TO YOU ABOUT YOUR PARENTS? GRANDPARENTS? ANCESTORS? IS THERE A FAMOUS PERSON IN YOUR FAMILY'S PAST?

5. ARE THERE ANY SPECIAL FAMILY RECIPES THAT HAVE BEEN HANDED DOWN FROM GENERATION TO GENERATION?

6. ARE FAMILY REUNIONS HELD AMONG MEMBERS OF YOUR FAMILY? HOW OFTEN? WHO COMES? ARE THERE RELATIVES YOU ARE HAPPY TO SEE? ONE'S YOU ARE UNHAPPY TO SEE?

7. HAVE YOU EVER BEEN THE VICTIM OF PREJUDICE AND/OR DISCRIMINATION? DESCRIBE THE SITUATION WHO WAS INVOLVED AND THEIR RACE. DESCRIBE YOUR EMOTIONS AND BODILY SENSATIONS.

8. HAVE YOU EVER OBSERVED PREJUDICE AGAINST OTHERS? WHAT DID YOU DO?

9. HAVE YOU EVER BECOME FRUSTRATED, ANGRY OR JUDG MENTAL WHEN TRYING TO COMMUNICATE WITH SOME ONE WHO DIDN'T SPEAK YOUR LANGUAGE?

10. HAVE YOU EVER AVOIDED PEOPLE OF A CERTAIN ETHNIC GROUP?

11. WHAT SLANG WORD HAVE YOU USED TO DESCRIBE MEM BERS OF YOUR RACE OR ANOTHER PERSON'S RACE, CUL- TURE OR RELIGION?

12. IF YOU COULD, WOULD YOU CHANGE YOUR RACE, RELI- GION, CULTURE AND/OR GENDER (MALE, FEMALE)?

This immigrant experience, written by Melba Alhonte, is very relevant for teachers working with children and parents from diverse cultures.

For many of us, coming to the United States from another country has been an extremely challenging experience. Most of us left our countries in order to fulfill the specific needs for:

- safety
- a higher standard of living
- freedom of religious expression
- rejoining specific family members
- education for our children
- education for ourselves
- adventure
- new career opportunities

While the United states offers many opportunities to fulfill these needs, we often neglect many of the needs that were naturally met while living in our original culture. Many of us were born into a Latin-American heritage that has imprinted us with the gifts of joy, humor and spontaneity. If our new culture doesn't support these natural qualities, they become unfulfilled needs which often leads to separation and pain.

BE UNFOLDED NOT MOLDED

The Anglo culture promotes important qualities such as hard work and self-sufficiency. In an effort to "fit in" there is a tendency to allow our new culture to mold us. It takes a great deal of awareness to allow our new culture to gracefully unfold our potential rather than being molded into people who have lost their soul. Some of us have become so focused on our desire to speak a new language that we have sacrificed the need to express who we are at a deep level. For many of us, Spanish is still the only language that allows us to share our reality and express our creativity in a way that affirms our sense of belonging. It is also very difficult to communicate with a sense of humor in a language that is not completely comfortable. Often, we are not even conscious that this "molding" is taking place, but inwardly it feels that something is dying inside.

Likewise, while the United States culture provides a great opportunity to achieve certain material goals, as Latin-Americans, some of us have neglected our need for community, family connection, affection, communication, and closeness. When we were young, the sounds, smells, flavors and colors of our environment were deeply imprinted in our essence. If these are not part of our present environment, there becomes a deep longing inside of us. For instance, I can remember the incredible joy and aliveness I felt the first time I walked through a Spanish speaking neighborhood in New York City on my way to teaching a class. Or, whenever I listen to the music of my childhood something comes alive inside of me. Unfortunately, many of us have neglected the influence and importance of these original experiences.

A powerful way to reclaim our childhood environment is to include objects in our homes and activities in our lives that remind us of the simple things that connect to our joy. A Caribbean parent spoke about reconnecting with her Island culture by going to a restaurant and ordering a whole grilled fish. Unfortunately, this rarely happened because her children only liked fast food. Another parent remembered how much she loved to dance. She had married into a family where dancing was not considered proper behavior for adults. In her culture every family event included dancing, even the elders in the family would joyfully dance. Once she gave up dancing, it was like a part of her was missing.

While participating in the class, both women decided to regain there love for life by reconnecting with those simple pleasures. The first decided to eat an entire fish whenever she could. The second joined a salsa class. It was important for them to fulfill those needs without any anger or judgment. These small decisions made a significant difference in the quality of their lives and as a result the whole family benefited.

Along the same lines, getting their kids to school on time had become an arduous task for many of the Parent Leadership Training participants. The experience become much more enjoyable once they had established relationships with other parents in the class. Now they look forward to enjoying a cup of coffee with their new friends after dropping their children off. The school was transformed from a cold institution to a friendly environment, by fulfilling their cultural need for creating community.

For many of my students that come from a warm tropical climate, the long cold winters with the absence of color and familiar sounds creates a state of low energy and great sadness. We recommend the use of colorful attire, and to create social settings that allow them to connect with others and feel less isolated. The intention is to do whatever it takes to "keep warm inside".

Small changes can make a big difference. Continually asking "What can I do to reconnect with the part of myself that loves life?" can totally transform the quality of your life. As we nurture and support ourselves at a deeper level, our life becomes richer and naturally leads to an exploration of passion and purpose. For many of us, these two qualities were most strongly felt when leaving our country of birth. Our hopes, dreams and fantasies for our future homeland provided a tremendous source of creativity and strength. Nothing was going to stop us from achieving this goal and purpose.

This powerful immigrant experience can serve as a reference point for reclaiming a sense of purpose. We can asks ourselves "What are we working towards now?" Is it a new career opportunity? Or advancing our level of education? Or, maybe our new goal is not a physical destination, but a new place inside of ourselves. A place where we can feel the joy of our past and the security of our present. A place where our needs on all levels are being met.

Each of us has a song in our hearts. They are all different and magnificent. It is by connecting inside with that energy that we are able to bring the world to a new level of consciousness.

VIVA LA DIFFERENCE

Everyone has something to give as well as something to learn. For example, in my Doctorate program many of my Anglo-American classmates are working on the need to connect to their sense of joy and fun. Whereas for me, freedom, spontaneity and joy are a part of my heritage and my focus has been discipline, and cultivating a logical way of thinking.

For most of the Latin-American parents this same loving and deeply caring approach to life and for each other comes naturally. Learning how to manifest in their new culture and better take care of themselves has become their focal point. Again, we all have something to give as well as something to learn.

VIVA LA EXPERIENCE

Some of the immigrant parents who participate in our programs express a lack of acceptance for the people and culture of the United States. This animosity is often the result of not acknowledging the grieving experience that is natural when leaving a native country and its culture. I have seen parents go from the numbness of denied nostalgia to celebrating the lessons their new country has to offer by becoming more aware of denied emotions. As we acknowledge and heal the pain we can better aid our children to integrate by being more open to the experiences that their new culture has to offer.

Studies have shown that children of diplomats, as well as others who are exposed on an on-going basis to diverse cultures, are better equipped to handle the challenges of our "global" society. After living in different cultures, these children are more aware of who they are, and are not handicapped by a "limited vision". They are able to empathize with cultural "truths", find a commonality among all people, and internalize the diverse gifts that each culture offers. For example, the Asian respect of elders or French love of philosophy.

Each culture on this planet has a gift, which metaphorically is a key. Our needs can be symbolized by a lock. By embracing these cultures, not on a superficial level, but on a deeper and significant level, we can unlock ourselves. In order to identify our needs, it is important that we go beyond "right" and "wrong"; beyond our comfort zones and the structures that were imposed upon us by those who cannot see beyond their limiting beliefs. We must also remember that life is full of learning experiences which will challenge us to use the keys to strengthen who we are.

EXERCISE

I.   WRITE DOWN THE SPECIAL AND IMPORTANT GIFTS OR

"KEYS" OF YOUR NATIVE CULTURE. (Ex-Joy, flexibility, sense of humor, beauty, love)

2. **WHAT ARE THE SPECIAL AND IMPORTANT GIFTS OR "KEYS" OF YOUR NEW CULTURE?** (Ex-honesty, reliability, success, the opportunity to advance, equality)

3. **HOW CAN YOU INTERGRATE THESE "KEYS" IN ORDER TO MAKE YOUR LIFE MORE FULLFILLING?**

4. UTILIZING YOUR CREATIVE IMAGINATION, SEE YOURSELF OWNING THESE GIFTS. HOW DOES IT FEEL?

5. WHAT SMALL CHANGES CAN YOU MAKE TO START MANIFESTING MORE OF THESE GIFTS?

CROSS-CULTURAL COMMUNICATIONS

EDUCATION FOR TRANSFORMATION

There are major differences in the communication styles of Latin-Americans and Anglo-Americans. This has been described as linear vs. circular communication. The circular style, used by Latin Americans, is more gentle and emphasizes the development of relationships. Whereas, the Anglo communication pattern is direct and has a goal in mind. Many Latin-Americans require this richer, emotional context rather than a direct linear approach in order to process information. In the Latin-American culture stories often are more effective than lists and bullets. Whereas, in the Anglo culture the opposite is more often the case. The linear approach places great importance on the concept of time. Many Anglo-Americans consider sitting around and just talking a total waste of time; whereas, for us, connecting through communication is essential.

In our programs, parents learn to interact more harmoniously by realizing that the Anglo culture places great value on doing whereas we are more concerned with relationship. For many immigrant parents, a teacher's objective evaluation of their child's academic performance is often interpreted emotionally as an attack rather than an opportunity to modify their child's behavior.

In these situations, we recommend that our parents translate the feed back from the emotional level of "You're child is not good enough" to the mental level of "Your child must do A, B, C to achieve D". This is not about right and wrong but about the subtleties of cultural diversity.

We also recommend, as a way of clearing the emotions, taking a walk, spending some time alone or talking to a neutral party before responding to an emotionally charged situation. When we can step back and reflect rather than react emotionally, our loving becomes less conditional and our life becomes more harmonious and productive. Also, our children will benefit by living in a home where challenging situations are dealt with in a mature, wise and successful manner.

EXERCISE

I. DESCRIBE A COMMUNICATION WHERE YOU HAD YOUR

FEELINGS HURT.

2. IS THERE A DIFFERENCE WHEN YOU OBJECTIVELY LOOK
   AT THE COMMUNICATION INSTEAD OF EMOTIONALLY
   REACTING TO THE INFORMATION? WAS THERE ANY VALUE
   IN WHAT WAS BEING COMMUNICATED? IF SO, WHAT WAS
   THE VALUE IN THE INFORMATION?

The corporate world is a product of the Anglo culture. It is extremely difficult for people who are not familiar with the linear way of communicat-

ing and thinking to advance in this area. Yet, there are people who have successfully transcended barriers that these communication differences can create. Instead of changing who they are in order to "fit in", they understand and respect the rules of each culture and are able to use them to their advantage. As an example, a Brazilian friend of mine was asked to represent her family's business at a meeting of the New York City textile industry. Upon arriving, she was so confident and full of life that, even though she broke all the "rules" of business, she won all the accounts.

Former president of the United States, Bill Clinton, is another person who understands and transcends cultural differences. Although he is linear in his thinking, he is able to adapt by not focusing solely on getting things done, but on the development of relationships as well. When he travels to Latin-America, he connects to the people of each country by spending time communicating personally and even by playing music with them.

In our workshops, we use cultural diversity as a catalyst for success. We need to remember that the multi-cultural, as well as all life experiences, can be used as tools to bring out more of who we are. As each experience melts together in the alchemy of life we become a stronger and more conscious individual.

I hope this material provided you with a deeper appreciation of the richness and potential of the multi-cultural experience. By going beyond judgments and viewing the world through acceptance, we realize that all of us have something to learn as well as something to give. As we embrace our new culture without sacrificing who we are, we grow as an individual and contribute to our children and the community in which we live.

HOME ASSIGNMENT #14

CULTURAL DIVERSITY

1. WRITE DOWN ALL THE POSITIVE AND NEGATIVE STEREO - TYPES YOU CAN THINK OF FOR:

    WHITES

    BLACKS

    PUERTO RICANS

    MEXICANS

    HOMOSEXUALS

    JEWS

    WOMEN

    MEN

    ASIANS

2. DEFEND A GROUP THAT YOU MIGHT HAVE NEGATIVE STEREO-TYPES ABOUT AS IF YOU WERE A MEMBER OF THAT GROUP.

EDUCATION FOR TRANSFORMATION

3. HOW DO YOUR CONDITIONED COGNITION'S (PREJUDICES) SUSTAIN RACISM, SEXISM AND/OR HOMOPHOBIA.

PARTICIPANTS COMMENTS

EDUCATION FOR TRANSFORMATION

- A mother was very concerned about her son's failing grades. The major reason for his poor academic performance was his inability to focus on his homework for more than ten minutes. At the same time he had many friends, and was well liked by peers as well as his teachers. I suggested that he include his need for social interaction as a way of improving his academic performance.

  Upon his mother's suggestion, he found a study partner who was a high academic achiever but who, interesting enough, did not have many friends. They complimented each other, and as a result his grades dramatically improved as he spent more time on doing his homework by creating a study environment where he was not alone.

- Another parent participant was having a problem at the hair salon where she worked. She was very extraverted and loved interacting with her clients. Unfortunately, her boss didn't value this trait and saw her ability to interact as a waste of time and money. This created so much stress that it was beginning to effect her health.

  After creating a support system in the class with parents who acknowledged potential, she was encouraged to open a salon in her home. She did this and as a result not only did she have more fun and earn considerably more money, but she also created jobs for two other people in the class.

- A father spent a great deal of class time complaining about problems that faced Latin-American people in his community. At one point, I asked him what he could practically do in order to channel his concern in a positive direction.

  He went out and asked people in his community which politicians supported his vision. He went to meetings and listened to what these politicians had to say. He eventually got a job working on one of their reelection campaigns.

- When my children grew up, I needed to find a situation to express my loving and nurturing in the world. I began by identifying my strengths and weaknesses. As part of growing up in a large family I enjoyed interacting with people. I was not a loner, and whatever I did would have to involve working with other people.

I also realized that, because of my compassionate nature, service had become a key motivator in my life. In that I had a tendency to loose focus, I needed to work with people who could direct me in expressing my natural ability to nurture and be of service in a very practical way.

Even though the focus was helping others, my first attempts were not fulfilling. I found that the people I was working with had too many structures and as a result stifled my creative expression. Their style did not allow me to bring my cultural instincts and who I was as a loving, spontaneous and creative woman into my working environment.

The process of writing this book, creating curriculum and presenting Parenting Programs, not only fulfills my need to serve others, but also takes place in an environment where my style and input are valued. I also get the clear direction that I need without being monitored too closely which has allowed my creativity and enthusiasm to flourish.

- A daughter's poor academic performance had become a source of tension and frustration for her mother. She had read the seemingly logical negative comments that her child's teacher had written on her last paper and totally took the teacher's feedback as the truth. As a result, her relationship with her daughter deteriorated, as her daughter had developed an aversion to school, and the home environment became a battle field.

Upon sharing her dilemma with the class, she began to see that the logical, lengthy and well thought out feedback that her daughter received from the teacher represented only one point of view.

Another point of view was that the information was basically critical with no clear direction provided. It became obvious to her that her daughter was being educated in a very linear way with no consideration given to her daughter's unique way of processing information.

At the next class she reported, "I spoke to her teacher and recommended that because my daughter is so visual, he use different colors to highlight his recommendations. Also, in that she was easily distracted, it would be helpful to give specific suggestions such as going to the library or another quiet place to work on projects."

I don't know the effect that the conversation had on her teacher, but I do know that I now acknowledge and respect my daughter's unique style of learning which has greatly improved our relationship."

CONTACT INFORMATION

Education for Transformation was developed and refined over the past eleven years to serve as the course text for our 40-hour Teachers Leadership Training. Participants receive Masters in Education credits upon successful completion of this program. Education for Excellence Inc. (Dr. Marc Rosenbaum, director) also presents the 18-hour Parents Leadership Training which is very similar in content to the program for educators. These programs have been presented to more than 3000 parents and teachers in New York City, California and Colombia. To find out more about our programs you can go to our website, www.ed4excellence.com.

To order copies of *Education for Transformation* please call 800-591-5988, go to our website, ask your local bookstore to order a copy, or go to any of the major online bookstores. If you have any feedback regarding the book or are interested in bringing the Parenting or Teachers programs to your area, please email marc@ed4excellence.com

221

CPSIA information can be obtained at www.ICGtesting.com
Printed in the USA
BVOW022010261212

309165BV00001B/2/A